Lette
Pra

Letters on
Prayer

MICHAEL PAUL GALLAGHER SJ

DARTON · LONGMAN + TODD

First published in 1994 by
Darton, Longman and Todd Ltd
1 Spencer Court
140–142 Wandsworth High Street
London SW18 4JJ

ISBN 0–232–52065–8

A catalogue record for this book is
available from the British Library

Scripture quotations are from *The Jerusalem Bible* (1966,
1967 and 1968) and *The New Jerusalem Bible* (1985), both
published by Darton, Longman and Todd Ltd and Doubleday Inc.

Thanks are due to The Dedalus Press for
permission to quote from 'The Fable of Being'
by Paul Murray in *The Absent Fountain*, and to the Benedictine
Community, Sacro Speco, Subiaco, Italy, for permission to reproduce
the *Adoration of the Magi* (Sienese School 14th century).

Phototypeset in 10/12½ Palatino by Intype, London
Printed and bound in Great Britain
at the University Press, Cambridge

Contents

Introduction

RELAXING AND REALISM

What is prayer? Many years ago, on a train to the north of Ireland, I hit upon an answer that has stayed with me. I was to give a retreat in Belfast. During the journey I decided to spend some time in prayer, and I wondered to myself, 'What am I really trying to do?' Almost at once a reply came: 'To pray is to relax into the reality of being loved by God.' Prayer after all need not be such an uphill effort. It is a way of remembering the One who embraces us, whether we realize it or not. In this sense I have often returned to those words that came to me on the train.

But now, years later, I would add a second half, and one that arose from a different setting. An important year of my life was spent in Latin America. I would have liked to continue there, but obedience had other plans. Like many others who have visited that continent, I found my spirituality being challenged and widened by the situation around me. In a world of such massive social divisions, and witnessing the aliveness of basic Christian communities, prayer changed its wavelength. Certainly, it involves relaxing into the reality of God's love, but it also means rising to the realism of loving like Christ.

On its own, the first half of my description might be too cosy. The second gives it grit, energy, purpose. Prayer involves a certain resting with God. But it should also make a difference to this world of woundedness. Sometimes we need to hear the first half, to learn to trust ourselves and God. At other moments we are ripe for the challenge of the second half: with changed hearts we can take our part in the building of the Kingdom here, in the slow transformation of our society. A good friend, deeply involved in work for justice, symbolizes for me how the two sides can be united. She told me that her prayer often takes the form of gazing at a crucifix, with the simple, repeated petition: 'Make me a companion of Your love.'

There is then a doubleness in prayer: an accent on trust followed by an accent on commitment. Indeed that rhythm is eloquently present in the 'Benedictus', the canticle of John the Baptist's father at the beginning of Luke's Gospel (Luke 1:68–79). It is a poem of praise in two long sentences. The first is an excited cry of joy over God's promise to 'visit' us, to free us from fear, to enable us to live 'in his presence, all our days', growing in love of God and of others ('holiness and justice'). The second sentence turns to the special calling of John the Baptist, or indeed of any of us: to liberate people by letting them know the compassion of God, which is compared to the dawn of each day as it ousts the dark of each night. I find this a great vision with which to begin the day and in fact it is always part of the morning prayer of the Church. First, we are offered an unexpected intimacy by God, and then we are sent into this world to bring healing and hope. Throughout the Bible nobody is ever called to be with God, full stop. God calls people into a new relationship and then sends them on a mission in the thick of reality.

These letters try to do justice to that doubleness in prayer, with its unity of trust and commitment. But above all they seek to stay close to experience and to the ordinary struggles encountered in prayer. They offer suggestions rather than solutions, and although they stem largely from issues raised by different individuals, I hope they may help other readers as well. Some of them began life in the monthly periodical *The Sacred Heart Messenger* (Dublin), but now they have been expanded and changed. Other letters have been added. But several important kinds of prayer get little attention here. For instance, since the focus is largely on personal prayer, not much is said about liturgical and communitarian aspects.

The aim is to offer practical encouragement to people who try to have some space of quiet for daily prayer. If prayer is remembering, in the pressures of everyday existence we all need some scaffolding for that remembering of the heart. We need structures, habits, patterns. Not necessarily techniques or methods in any narrow sense. These letters try to meet a range of difficulties raised by people, and provide support for their adventure in prayer. Everyone's situation is different. Everyone's path of prayer is surely as individual as their fingerprint. Any wisdom in this book has been learned or adapted from others. I simply pass it on, and add occasionally some insights forged from my own attempts to pray.

Letter 1

GETTING STARTED

Dear Liz and Brian,

You ask me about prayer and also to tell you something of my own prayer. Well, to begin with, I *try* to pray every day. But some days I only go through the motions. I imagine you know the experience because you say you've both been putting some time aside for prayer each day for some months now. I think that's marvellous, and it's all the more so because you are trying it as a couple.

Of course, your individual experiences will be different but there is huge support in the fact that you are both committed to some daily space for prayer. I love the idea that sometimes you do it together, just sitting in silence in the same place. 'Even if it is only ten minutes', you add. But ten minutes is ten minutes, and it mounts up day by day. Some days, as I was saying from my own experience, can seem to be total failures: you're just there, without focus, and it ends up seeming empty.

I've come to the conclusion that how I start off – within the first few minutes – is crucial. It can influence the whole period of prayer. One of the recurring faults in my own prayer is when I forget this and start without

1

real focus or real reverence. I remember an old priest saying to me years ago, when I had confessed to being distracted in prayer, 'But how could you be distracted, if you remember you are in the presence of God?' It sounded too simple, and perhaps it was. But a secret is there. Without some deliberate rudder I stray. In fact psychologists say that the first few minutes of a conversation or meeting set a tone and influence the whole interaction between people. Something similar is true of prayer, at least to gather the attention. God's attention to us is total (a strange truth). But we need to direct the heart, because otherwise we fall into the forgetfulness and drift that is part of most lives.

In this letter I want to tell you a few of my discoveries about this business of getting started properly. It's like someone learning to drive a car: at first it's always awkward and jerky, co-ordinating the brake and the gears and the accelerator. But then you get used to it, and it becomes second nature. I'm not sure whether these little helps for prayer ever become second nature as in driving. But they are like those initial moves you make to get underway.

The first ingredient, I think, is self-patience – because often it takes time to reach the quiet level of listening that is the key to personal prayer. Don't be surprised if you find yourself 'all over the place' when you try to be still. It sometimes reminds me of those snow scenes in water containers that used to be popular around Christmas time. The flakes would fall everywhere when you moved the jar. But after a time they would settle again. The beginning of prayer usually needs some patience before quiet comes.

There are many helpful ways of creating this quiet, *if* it does not arrive naturally. So my second ingredient

2

So far everything has been about gathering the self into stillness, about how *we* can be more ready for prayer. But prayer involves God. How do you think of God, to whom you come in prayer? That's another crucial question which influences how you approach the whole adventure of trying to pray. Some years ago I heard Anthony de Mello speaking about prayer. He has his own striking way of putting things. He asked people what God they prayed to. Is God sulky? Someone who turns away in bad humour because you have been less than perfect in your relationship? De Mello contrasted this Judgement God with what he called the God of Welcomes. I can still remember him describing God getting excited like a child because *you* are coming to pray. 'God has all these angels with golden trumpets. They are to get ready to welcome you. God has this infinite red carpet: roll it out, he says to another group of angels.' And de Mello ended by challenging his audience. 'You think my pictures are silly and childish. I tell you, they are much more true than the images you may have, especially if you have some picture in the back of your head of a distant and bored and sulky God.'

Perhaps even after years of theology studies, false pictures of God can still lurk in our imaginations, so that we too become false. We put on prayer masks. We do our religious duty. We try to bargain with this Boss or placate this Judge. We have forgotten that the Lord takes delight in people. In more ordinary language, God is 'thrilled' to see us.

So get yourselves ready patiently. But remember the true God of love to whom you come. Then, some days at least, those ten minutes of yours can flow naturally and easily, and most importantly of all, leave you strengthened for a life of love.

Letter 2

COPING WITH DIFFICULTIES IN PRAYER

From the reply of Liz and Brian: Your letter helped us a lot. It's not easy to get God right with all those strange gods in our heads. And the methods for creating inner quiet can be essential on more chaotic days.

You may be interested to know that we have discovered that our ways of praying are quite different but still we find it a great help to do it at the same time, sitting in the same place, and afterwards we sometimes talk about it. We try to keep the same time – after the evening meal. The kids clear things up (usually!) and we go into the small spare room. By the way, they know that we go for 'meditation together' and sometimes they ask about it.

We start by reading a short passage of Scripture. Years ago we went to a course on the Bible and it opened our eyes to this book as a foundation for our faith. For our daily prayer even a sentence or two can be enough. We take turns in choosing it. After that it's silence for ten to fifteen minutes and whoever did not read the passage at the beginning, reads it aloud at the end. We stand and, holding hands, say an Our Father and Hail Mary together. And that's it.

Except that sometimes one of us wants to share something.

What goes on during the silence? Brian is more inclined to be quiet and simply to think of God – perhaps using a Psalm phrase as you suggested. He says that he needs to give more attention to the quietening down exercises you suggested in your letter. Liz prefers Gospel scenes and likes to enter into them in a conversational way, bringing herself into the episode of healing or whatever. She finds that by visualizing herself in the scene, she can make it personal.

We don't always manage to keep this daily prayer appointment. If we miss it for a few evenings running, it shows in other areas of life. Grumpiness increases. Real communication is avoided. So sooner or later we get back to it. But even when we 'do' it, we have times when we wonder whether prayer has any point at all. We hang in there but it's frustrating, empty, without focus. What can you say to keep us going? What might help us when any effort to try to gather oneself seems just a mess and gets nowhere? Because, to be honest, we sometimes feel like throwing in the sponge. If we were not doing it together, we might have thrown it in long ago! And yet we do know over time that without this little effort, our lives would be much the poorer. So tell us a bit more about how to cope with those 'bad days'.

Dear Liz and Brian,

I've no doubt that your strongest support comes from one another. I think many couples *could* do what you do, but perhaps few manage to pray together like that. Your perseverance becomes much easier because of your joint commitment as a couple. Like a joint bank account! You're both responsible for it. It's a question of what I like to call 'scaffolding' or what the old philosophers would call a 'habit'. Modern life-style is strong on distractions. Unless I have some regular slots in which I turn towards God no matter how I feel, the whole thing can be far too haphazard for any steady growth. Too innocent in fact. In a sense you answered your question yourselves: the courage to hold on to the 'habit' is the first way of overcoming the 'bad days'.

Still the frustrations you mention are very real. I have no magic solution, simply a few suggestions that have sometimes helped me when prayer seemed useless or impossible. Four suggestions in fact.

The first is to be more careful (when times are 'bad') about laying the foundations of listening. When the going is rough you may need to give more time to those skills of stillness mentioned in my previous letter. They build up an attitude of reverence for the God towards whom I try to turn in prayer. Even posture can help us to remember-with-reverence to Whom we come. If there is some sense of emptiness, slouching will only add to it. Indeed the whole oriental tradition is much stronger on the role of the body in prayer. But the outer reverence is only an expression of an inner attitude: this encounter, called prayer, is different from anything else in our experience simply because God is God. A little care at the outset can help to do justice to this uniqueness. Indeed I make those 'bad days' worse when I take the whole business for granted, and forget the receptive readiness I need to enter into the dialogue called prayer.

A second possibility is to return to some favourite Scripture passage that gave you nourishment in the past. Just because you start from a particular piece of Scripture each evening need not mean that it has to be the only focus for your prayer. If things are empty, go back to where they were once full. Revisiting a moment of grace is very helpful – especially when things are 'a mess' as you say. We all have 'core memories' that are central to our faith story – just as the Exodus liberation remained at the centre of the Old Testament experience of God. Our personal memories can be of many kinds. They can range from an event like one's first communion as a child to more adult moments of emerging from some period of darkness into new light.

Another way of coping with confusion is simply to admit honestly how I am. If I'm feeling angry, or lost, or despairing, or exhausted, or just uninterested in trying to reach out to God, it's a real and humble prayer to express it all to the Lord. The Psalms are full of negative feelings of this kind: 'Has his love vanished for ever?' (76); 'My heart is full of fear' (143); 'I am like the dumb unable to speak' (37); 'My God you give no reply – I find no peace' (21). And often in those Psalms, such voicing of pain opens a path towards rediscovering trust in God. Sometimes the negative feelings have God as their target. In a time of hurt or mourning, prayer can be blocked by a secret fear of offending God by some expression of anger. Again the example of the Psalms pushes us towards a naked honesty that does not shirk from accusing God: 'How long will you turn away your face from me? How long must I nurse rebellion in my soul?' (2); 'You have turned my friends and neighbours against me, now darkness is my one companion left' (88). As in the deepest kinds of human friendship (think of your own marriage), one can express such disappointment and churned up emotions without fear of not being accepted.

Finally, I think of a saying from St Catherine of Siena: what matters in prayer is not feeling-during but loving-after. In other words the test is love. I don't pray just to feel good. That's only partly true: of course the 'child' in me wants instant comfort, but the adult can embrace a deeper agenda of dark trust. It's a great help to have

9

some consolation but the deeper purpose is that I learn to love. And so when things are dark or numb, pray for others. Remember the many places of struggle and suffering in the world and be there with them and for them before God. I'm often surprised how quickly the personal clouds can lift when I recall the situation of so many others and try to pray for them. Remember the very first word of the Lord's Prayer: it is not just about 'me'.

I'm convinced that we all need some ways like these to survive those 'bad days'. They are not easy to put into practice, but they can give courage to cope, and may even help to turn difficulties into occasions for growth in trust and in love.

Letter 3

FIRST STEPS IN PERSONAL PRAYER

When these two letters were published in the Irish spiritual monthly The Messenger, *this comment came from Tony: I don't want to complain but your letters on prayer to that married couple were a bit beyond me. They had done courses on Scripture and have years of praying behind them. I'm just a young man who sometimes drops into the church for a few minutes on the way home from work. I only say prayers, like the Our Father, that I learned as a child, and I add a kind of hello and goodbye to God. What else would you advise?*

Dear Tony,

What you say is real and honest, and also a great basis for growth. You seem like someone who is able to swim already, but wants to do a bit of further training. For me the real key is something you already have but don't really say in your letter. You have a sense of God (which leads you to 'drop in' to the church) and a desire to deepen your way of praying (that pushed you to write). That faith and that desire are more important than any suggestions I may make here. Without those two pillars, all the books on prayer in the world would simply be useless.

But yes, I'd like to mention ways of building on what you already have. For instance, you seem to have a friendly approach to God – the 'hello and goodbye' you mention. Trust that and expand on it – praying in your own way and in your own words. That's something I'll come back to, perhaps in another letter.

There is nothing wrong with those childhood prayers. How could we ever improve on the 'Our Father'? What matters is how we say it. The easiest way to 'improve' is just to take your time. I think it's much better to say this great prayer as slowly as you can, pausing on each phrase, than to say it rapidly many times.

Recently I was present at a mass when the priest invited the congregation to make two gestures during the Lord's Prayer. For the first half they were asked to raise their arms above their shoulders, as if reaching out towards the Father beyond us. Then during the second half they were to lower the arms to waist level, keeping their hands open, as if in a gesture of petition and of need for themselves and others. Those gestures brought out a change between the two halves of the Our Father: at first we pray about God's reality and vision of things, and then we turn to our own humbler reality and needs.

Perhaps because we learn that prayer of Jesus as children, even as adults we may be saying deep words that we have never paused to examine. I won't try to offer you a detailed commentary on each phrase. Instead I want to paraphrase the prayer in more modern language and to write it out as a little personal meditation – so as to suggest the richness behind those very familiar words.

OUR FATHER
Jesus dared to call You 'Daddy', 'Abba'.
You are a tender parent,
like a loving mother or father,
something I forget so easily,
making You impersonal, distant, cold.
And You are '*Our* Father'.
It only seems that I pray alone.
I am with so many others,
all as sisters and brothers,
everyone, everywhere.
Thinking of what I have seen on TV news in recent
    days,
remembering anyone whom I saw today,
even strangers, passing by,
can I truly realize that he or she is another child of
    You, 'Our Father'?
WHO ART IN HEAVEN, HALLOWED BE THY
    NAME
You are also beyond us all – ('in heaven').
I ask you to realize and reverence
Your otherness from us – (to 'hallow' You),
to recognize the greatness and beauty that is You,
to know who You really are – ('Thy name')
in mystery and in intimacy.
THY KINGDOM COME
You have huge hopes for us,
what Jesus described in His stories
as a slow change of government in the heart,
a different approach to everything,
the coming of Your Kingdom.
Jesus spoke of it as a tiny seed
that slowly, silently, in darkness and in day,
becomes a shelter-giving tree.

13

Or like the surprise of a treasure stumbled across,
so that the finder wants to give up everything
in order to own that field with its secret.
Or like an expert jeweller
on the look-out for years for a special pearl,
and when the perfect pearl is found,
there is such joyful freedom that any price will be
    paid.
May that seed find roots in me,
growing into a tree of care
where others can find some shelter.
May I know the surprise of the treasure,
and the delight of the long-sought pearl,
and then the heart-freedom
to live this revolution
You call Your Kingdom.
THY WILL BE DONE ON EARTH,
AS IT IS IN HEAVEN
You have a plan for our lives to be
healed with love, even here 'on earth'.
There are some situations that I can't change:
even in these may I live in tune with You,
because You can bring forth fruit,
where I can see no point or possibility.
May I face and embrace without resentment,
these painful realities around me and within me.
And where I am free to choose or change,
may I find and follow Your hopes for me,
but trust in Your wisdom
for all I can't control.
GIVE US THIS DAY OUR DAILY BREAD
Without Your help I can't live Your vision:
I need strength of many kinds,
nourishment for the journey of this day.

Our whole world is hungry and full of cries:
give us the bread of Your Spirit
so we may better share the bread of this planet.
AND FORGIVE US OUR TRESPASSES
AS WE FORGIVE THOSE WHO TRESPASS
  AGAINST US
But I damage myself by lack of love,
by forgetting to grow, by narrowing the heart.
Look on me with a love that heals my hardness,
and melts my resistance.
Then let your liberation flow
through me, towards others,
so that I echo and pass on your healing,
and share the courage of your compassion,
forgiving both the smaller hurts of every day,
and the bigger wounds that weigh on the memory.
AND LEAD US NOT INTO TEMPTATION
I started by glimpsing Your greatness
and end now recognizing my fragility.
There are danger zones for me,
when I can forget You and Your way.
I don't ask to be cushioned from any challenge,
but only to see through the traps,
and to grow in the tussle with tough choices.
BUT DELIVER US FROM EVIL
Protect me in the struggles of each day,
and against the deeper and long-term deceptions.
From the nonsense and the lies
within us and around us, set us free.
Against the evil enthroned in our world,
destroying us with comforts or with deprivations,
set us free,
help us not to sleep
but to struggle for your kind of justice.

Liberate us for fullness of life,
and for Your great hopes. Amen.

PS After writing all that, I came across the following
comment on the Our Father in an Italian book by Adri-
ana Zarri. I think what she says balances out what might
be too narrow or subjective in what I have written. She
gave me an excellent insight into how the Our Father is
much more than a prayer of personal petition.

To all appearances the Our Father is a prayer of
petition. But it really asks for few things (bread,
pardon, help in temptation). The other parts only
seem to be petitions.

We ask that God's kingdom come, but we know
well that the kingdom will come. We ask that God's
will be done, but we know well that it is always
fulfilled . . . God has promised so much, and if we
ask for those promises to be kept, it seems like a
lack of faith. In fact these phrases are more than
petitions. They are expressions that are more true
on the level of feelings than of reason. Like when
we tell a person whom we love that we do indeed
love him or her. We know that the expression has
meaning, not on the level of communicating infor-
mation: it is an exclamation, a cry from the soul.

Likewise with 'thy Kingdom come, thy will be
done'. It is mainly a joyful confession of faith and a
loving surrender to God's love . . . This is a prayer
of supreme 'uselessness' on the level of petition,
perhaps because it is so much more than a petition. Or rather, as the element of petition fades, it
gives way to something else: to adoration, surrender,
union with the Holy Spirit, who prays in us and in

16

us speaks with the Word and the Father, in a total freedom of love.

Letter 4

RESENTMENT AND OTHER ENEMIES

Tony wrote back after a few weeks: I did as you said and took the Our Father very slowly. I was surprised to find how real it could be. When I came to the words about forgiving us as we forgive others, it was too close for comfort. You see, for some time I've had a difficult relationship with one of the supervisors at work, a bossy type who gives me a hard time, and seems to have it in for me in particular. I needn't go into the details but sometimes when I visit that church on the way home, and try to be quiet, I just realize how churned up I am, even bitter. It's hard to pray then. But what you said about the Our Father forced me to see that I have to face it, and ask to forgive that man in my heart. Otherwise the prayer is all wrong, isn't it?

And the other discovery I made is that sometimes I don't really want to pray. I drop into the church out of routine. But I'm tired inside. The flame of my faith is very low, and I leave after a few minutes of struggle. What would you suggest for those empty days?

Dear Tony,
Well done! You've made a few important discoveries. I

think you've hit on two really important areas in prayer. You're right. You can't pray genuinely if you are *clinging* to some bitterness or anger. Notice how I put that. It's sometimes impossible to *feel* forgiving and positive towards a difficult person. But forgiving is possible in spite of feelings – at least in the sense of trying to understand and not to 'harden the heart' as the Bible so often says.

Above all, as I said, try not to cling to the resentment. Bring it before God, who knows that other person, and you may find even your feelings gradually healed. One exercise that could help is to look for various reasons why that supervisor may be so difficult. It involves stepping into his shoes, so to speak, with some sympathy or imagination. He has his burdens to carry. You may be able to guess some of them. The aim is to enter, prayerfully, into his world for a moment. If you can even begin to see him as Christ does, you may be less harsh on him in your own mind. 'Bossy types' for instance are often afraid of losing control, of not being respected. They feel they have to act tough, or else they may seem weak. Listen to the lonely pain in such a person. If you glimpse something like this in him, it does not mean that his treatment of you is justified, but perhaps it becomes more understandable. It does not mean that your own tensions disappear, but perhaps you need not react so strongly.

I don't for a moment think that any of this is easy. It's slow. But you can decide to fight bitterness, to try to let go of any animosity, and more important still, you can ask for the grace to forgive more fully and deeply.

Come back to the bigger horizon of the Our Father. That phrase about forgiveness seems to suggest a dangerous bargain – asking God to imitate me! St Paul, however, puts it the other way round: 'The Lord has forgiven you; now you must do the same' (Colossians 3:13). So we are asked to imitate God's compassion. It's two-way traffic, where the main flow starts from God. Something deep is at stake here, something crucial for being a Christian.

If you refuse to share God's love of somebody else, then you are blocking your own receiving of that love in prayer. You are stopping the flow of that love from reaching out through you towards someone else. But remember that love is more a question of decision than of warm feelings.

If you brood on your hurts or worse, if you nurse your grudges, then your prayer will be half-hearted, and – as far as the Our Father is concerned – dishonest. But often if you make even the slightest effort to let go of the natural (and even justified) anger, or, as I suggested, to understand perhaps the tense personality of that other man, and the pressures on him, it can work wonders. Any step in the right direction and you may find that the flow of prayer opens up again.

Tony, you put your finger on something that many people run into, except that they can miss the connection between a resentment they won't let go of and an inability to pray. But, as you found out, the Our Father suggests a deep link between our relationship to God and our relationship to others. Because prayer and life are never neatly separate. They always influence one another, for better or worse, and growth in one means growth in the other. And surprisingly, life – the quality of how you live each day – has perhaps a more direct influence on prayer – on how you contact God – than prayer has on life.

Prayer Is More Than Your Doing

Your other question also raises a problem for most of us – that sense of not having the inner energy to pray and perhaps not really wanting to. I have no magic answer. You have seen what I wrote to Liz and Brian about their uphill or blocked times in prayer. Apart from the practical approaches I suggested to them, let me add a general attitude that can help on what you call 'empty days'. Prayer involves more than you alone. I've just been saying that my attitude to other people is intimately connected with prayer. But there is another relationship involved: that with God, of course. The flame of your faith may be weak – as you put it – but the flame of God's faith in you is more important and never weak.

Perhaps that sounds great but a bit distant. So make it concrete. Think of the famous scene in the Gospel about Zacchaeus (from Luke 19). Nowadays in school children love to perform it as a little drama, climbing the tree and so on. And even small children, in their own way, can understand that this is a story of two desires, a weak desire and a strong desire. Zacchaeus wants to see Jesus, but perhaps just out of curiosity. But Jesus wants to find him and even stay at his house. Do you see the parallel? When you or I are feeling only vaguely interested in prayer, it's like Zacchaeus hiding, as I imagine, in the leaves of the tree, perhaps afraid of being seen or recognized. But he changes as soon as he knows that someone wants him, recognizes him, and even loves him. The story is about two kinds of searching, and about what happens, beyond any question of merit, when Jesus enters a person's life.

So when those 'useless days' come, and they will come, remember Whom you are approaching in prayer: the One who approaches you. Try to change the focus,

21

realizing how the Lord wants to reach out to you, even when you feel no desire to reach out to him. Give it a little time and you may get beyond that 'useless' feeling. From those tired moments you learn that prayer is God's doing. You have to be a little understanding of yourself, and like John the Baptist, prepare the way of the Lord. That change of wavelength is easier said than done. But it's the invitation of God that counts – like Jesus inviting himself into the house of the surprised Zacchaeus.

Letter 5

GETTING SOMETHING
OUT OF IT

It might sound like my teenage children, writes Eileen, but am I meant to get something out of prayer? If I am, I'm not sure what it is. I feel a duty to pray, to honour God, to ask a blessing on our family and so on. Recently I heard someone interviewed on the radio and he was talking about experiencing God as consolation each day. Am I missing something?

Dear Eileen,

I think many people will echo your question. My simple answer would be: yes, perhaps there is more to prayer than you were brought up to expect.

But isn't that true of many things? When, early one October morning, I took vows as a Jesuit, at the age of twenty-four, I thought I understood them inside out. After two years of stern noviciate reflection, I knew it all! And then with the years I've found out much more – in the school of life. Living those promises is deeper and tougher and more joyful than I imagined at the outset. Indeed these middle years of life (which you are just entering) bring what has been called 'the sacrament of self-defeat'. I'm not going to be the kind of saint I planned, but some less dramatic and more modest sanctity may be God's hope for me.

Perhaps you could say the same looking back on your wedding. It had its imagined ideals and then came the slow reality of the years, itself a precious place for the heart to learn. So why be surprised if our relationship to God also changes and expands with the passing of time?

Your question has to do with the 'fruits' of prayer. Are we meant to be different because we try to pray? Surely the answer is yes. As I write, we are in the season of the year between Easter and Pentecost. It's all about new life in Christ and the gifts of the Spirit. It's not just something way back in history – at the beginning of Christianity. It's a reality offered to each of us now, and prayer is the key to making it real in the flow of life.

You mentioned the person on the radio who was talking about 'consolation' through prayer. That can mean enjoying God's presence, even with quiet and deep feelings of joy. Or it can mean something less special and more ordinary – finding strength to live the Christian life with its daily receivings and givings.

In 1993 we celebrated the fourth centenary of the birth of George Herbert, an Anglican minister who was also a great poet. He once wrote a sonnet on prayer. It's famous in the world of literature for having no sentences, just phrases that describe prayer in many different ways. Some of them evoke prayer as petition, as a battering ram against the Almighty. Some of them compare prayer to hearing heavenly music. I think that Herbert is deliberately giving eloquent descriptions in order to surprise us with his simple conclusion. The last words of the poem are 'something understood'. (The sonnet is quoted in full at the end of the letter.)

24

I like that. It suggests that when we pray the heart learns something in its own strange way. Even if the going is tough. Even if I don't feel much. Perhaps only at the end is 'something understood'. I don't think Herbert means that I have worked something out with the mind. Instead I have understood something more deeply and on another level – about God, or about love, or about myself, or about others. A glimpse of love that gives food for living.

Do I get something out of prayer? Yes, my horizon expands and attitudes get healed by being in the presence of God. So an important fruit of prayer is genuine peace and the courage to love. And this can happen even without strong feelings.

Let me put it another way. In the famous scene of the annunciation in Luke 1, which has prayer at its core, notice the drama of Mary's change of attitude. At first she is described as 'deeply disturbed' by the messenger. Perhaps we forget this moment of panic and struggle, because so many artists have shown the scene in beautiful golden light. They show it as a scene of pure consolation. That is true, but it comes later. It comes after questioning ('how can this be?'), listening ('The Holy Spirit will come'), and surrendering ('let it be done'). Indeed we could say that Mary arrives at 'something understood'; she understands something extraordinary at the centre of human history. And she understands, after that initial panic, something of her own key role in God's hopes.

I think our prayer can often have the same pattern: confusion, searching, listening, acceptance, something understood in the heart. Something about God, and about what God wants of me now.

Go to the other end of the Gospels and you can see a

25

similar pattern in the resurrection scenes. Isn't it striking
how Jesus shows himself to his friends at moments when
they are 'down', as we say nowadays? Locked in the
upper room because of fear. Mary Magdalene weeping
her eyes out because the body is gone. Walking away in
disillusionment – back to Emmaus. Or take the great
scene at the end of John's Gospel: the story of Jesus
showing himself at the lakeside (John 21:1–8). It comes
at a moment of failure. These experienced fishermen
have spent a whole night without catching anything at
all! When they heed his voice on the shore, all changes.
He suggests that they try casting the net another way.
Suddenly that net is full, more full than ever before.

All these are stories of emerging from darkness into
light, from emptiness to fullness. As St Ignatius of Loyola
liked to stress, the Risen Lord comes always as consoler.
And yes, prayer can repeat that drama, as those stories
echo again and again in our lives. We can and should
expect to receive consolation or strength for the journey
– to get something out of it. Not in some extraordinary
way of hearing voices. Not in any childish way of wanting self-satisfaction. Not focusing on results: the core of
prayer is somehow being with God. But being with God
has effects on us, side-effects if you like. We find ourselves changed and set free to live in everyday love. We
find ourselves over the years becoming a bit more like
God – in spite of, or even because of that 'sacrament of
self-defeat'. Because as one of the parables puts it, the
seed grows even while the sower sleeps: night and day
it grows, we know not how (Mark 4:27). Even when you
seem to pray in the dark, just as when you see your way
in the light, growth goes on. Something is understood.
More importantly, something is being lived.

A quick remark before I close. In your letter you were

talking about prayer as a 'duty'. That's a slightly cold word. It can suggest a distant or cold God. If it's only a 'duty' in this sense, then prayer could suffer from low expectations. It could seem as if I'm left to myself, and as if I have caught nothing all night, full stop. But there is a Stranger on the shore, inviting me to try the other side. And the Stranger has great expectations of what he wants me to find . . .

PS *Prayer*

Prayer the Church's banquet, Angel's age,
God's breath in man returning to his birth,
The soul in paradise, heart in pilgrimage,
The Christian plummet sounding heav'n and
    earth:
Engine against th'Almighty, sinners' tower,
Reversed thunder, Christ-side-piercing
    spear,
The six days world transposing in an hour,
A kind of tune, which all things hear and fear;
Softness and peace and joy, and love, and
    bliss,
Exalted Manna, gladness of the best,
Heaven in ordinary, man well drest,
The milky way, the bird of paradise,
Church-bells beyond the stars heard, the
    soul's blood,
The land of spices: something understood.
George Herbert

Letter 6

THE SPIRIT PRAYS
WITHIN US

Dear Eileen,

You have another question, shorter but not easy. 'What is the core of prayer?' you ask. 'Is it asking for what I want or is it simply being with God? Or something else?'

Petition or presence? Let's see what the Gospels say. I'm sure you remember how Jesus praised a certain stubbornness in prayer, when he described someone determined to get a friend to open the door even during the night. That's our side of it – as if we sometimes have to keep on knocking in the dark of night. But Jesus went on to touch on God's side of it: will a good parent give a child something harmful? If the child wants an egg, will a parent give him or her a scorpion? (By the way, years ago in India the meaning of this came home to me in a new way: one night I found a scorpion in my room and when asleep it can look like an egg!) That Gospel passage goes on: if human parents try to give their children what is best for them, 'how much more will the heavenly Father give the Holy Spirit'. (All this is in chapter 11 of Luke's Gospel.)

Perhaps we have many small needs (even though very

real), but in fact only one big need – to receive Christ's Spirit. So one answer to your question about petition or presence would be: 'both are needed – don't separate them.' Even if you are praying, for instance, for a successful operation for a friend, you are also asking for the presence of the Spirit for that friend – and for yourself.

As it happens next month (June) brings together three feasts in the Catholic Church that can offer further light on your questions: Pentecost, Trinity, and the Sacred Heart.

Sometimes people say, 'It would have been marvellous to be in Palestine when Jesus was there – then I would have no difficulty believing or praying'. Maybe they forget how unsteady in faith the disciples were – until the day of Pentecost. That was when everything changed for them.

At the Last Supper Jesus spoke about sending them a new gift – the Paraclete. The original Greek word means several things: consoler, helper, protector, intercessor or defence lawyer. Indeed Jesus says that the presence of the Spirit will be 'another' Paraclete for us: in other words, Jesus himself was our first friend and defender, but now the Spirit will continue his work in an even more intimate way – both 'with you' and 'in you' in the words of the Gospel (John 14:17). It is as if all of us believers are on trial before the hostile court called the 'world', but we are not left defenceless. The Paraclete will be *beside* us, like a good advocate. Even more importantly, the Spirit will be *within* us to keep our hearts in tune with Christ and able to pray in the different circumstances of life.

St Paul brings out even more strongly the role of the Spirit in our prayer. In a famous passage in Romans he says: 'The Spirit too comes to help us in our weakness.

For when we cannot choose words in order to pray properly, the Spirit himself expresses our plea in a way that could never be put into words' (8:26). The Spirit prays in us – when we can't find the right wavelength. Not only that, the Spirit 'groans' with us – as if in pain or struggling. I've always been struck by a remark of Patrick White (the Nobel prize-winning Australian novelist) that the Church can be so complacent and banal about suffering. Not so the Spirit. There is pain, darkness, confusion in every life, and sometimes agonies inexpressible. The Spirit carries all this beyond our words in that 'groaning'.

Nothing could be more genuinely consoling, I think. Nor more real for many people who run into blankness and deserts in prayer from time to time. To go back to your question: the Spirit is both presence and petition *within* you. And especially when all goes wrong, and you seem weak, wordless and numb.

What about the Trinity? It's sad that so many people think of it as a distant theory, a 'mystery' that they accept but that makes no difference to them. I think the Trinity has a huge relevance for prayer. Remember the prayers of the mass. Whom are we praying to? The Father. Whom are we praying with? Jesus – 'through him, with him, in him'. Who is praying in us? The Spirit.

In all this I'm helped by something I noticed in India years ago. If you ask a child in the East where God is, he or she will point to their heart – to God within us. If you ask a child in our part of the world, most likely they will point up towards the sky – to God beyond us. Both answers are right and Christian, but there is a third Christian answer – we can point to God beside us, present in each person.

Point upwards yes, as an inadequate way of symbolizing God the Father whom nobody has seen (John 1:18). Point inwards as meaning the shy and yet powerful indwelling of the Spirit 'poured into our hearts' (Romans 5:5). But point around you also to the sacrament of the other person, for Jesus says we will find him there in a special way: 'as often as you did so even to the least of mine, you did so to me' (Matthew 25:40).

Your question was about presence. The Trinity means (among many other things) that God is present to us in three ways – the Father beyond us whom we have never seen, the Son beside us in humanity, and the Spirit deep within us.

How does this link with prayer in practice? The Gospel describes how Jesus often prayed at night on the hills of Palestine. You can picture your prayer in this light: it is as if you are *with* Jesus on the mountain, where he prayed *to* the Father, and the Spirit prayed *within* him. So you too are guided by the Spirit to be with Jesus before the Father. Seen in this way, the Trinity can become more central in prayer.

Perhaps for most people, most of the time, prayer means keeping their eyes on Jesus and on his humanity. This brings me to the third feast I mentioned. So much can be said about the Sacred Heart. It is an important Catholic devotion that has fallen a bit from favour, and often remains a closed book not only to Christians of other traditions, but many Catholics too. To all I would say: don't be put off by some of the awful pictures. There is a deep reality here. Pause on those two familiar words – sacred heart. Put together, they mean quite simply that our God is a God who feels. In the heart of Jesus we see the vulnerable side of God. In Him we have someone who knows the pain of loving and getting no response. So when confusion comes, when feelings are hurt, when

31

all seems to be churned up, to focus, in this sense, on the heart of Jesus puts you in touch with One who shares your struggles of heart – and also invites you to share the concerns of his heart.

There are three very different moods that influence prayer: times of serene quiet; times of emotional upheaval; times of tired emptiness. I need to approach God differently depending on what state I happen to be experiencing.

When all is easy and silent, I can adore the Trinity, that community of divine lovers.

When all is troubled, I can share it with the heart of Jesus.

When everything is blank or 'all over the place', I trust that the Spirit can find a language of prayer that makes up for my weakness.

Perhaps in the light of these feasts, I glimpse how marvellously varied our adventure of meeting God in prayer can be.

Letter 7

SCRIPTURE AND PRAYER

I have a shameful confession to make, writes Padraig. I do try to pray but I'm very ignorant about the Scriptures. I don't even have a Bible of my own. In my generation it wasn't 'the thing'. At school we weren't encouraged in this direction. But now I often take home the Sunday mass leaflet, and occasionally I find myself hooked, so to speak, on some phrase or passage of the readings. Recently for instance, I liked a sentence in Isaiah: 'as a mother comforts a child, so I shall comfort you' (66:13). Two Sundays running we had passages from Luke's Gospel, one about the Good Samaritan and the other about Martha and Mary. I was struck by the difference. One seems to say, be active. The other says, be quiet. Where do I go from here? How could I approach Scripture in a more personal and prayerful way?

Dear Padraig,
Don't worry – you're not alone in your 'shameful confession' that you are weak in your acquaintance of the Bible. But now various passages in mass readings have whetted your appetite. What might be the next step? That's an important question.

First of all, I don't think it's a matter of study or becoming more expert from reading much *about* the

Bible. Something in that direction could be a great help but it's not the key to what you are asking. Let's start from what you know: some passages read at Sunday mass. Yes, even with these, it is possible to develop a way of listening to God speaking to *you* in the Scriptures.

Do you really believe that last sentence? Or better, have you ever experienced the reality of God addressing you? Because that's *the* springboard for praying with Scripture. God speaks to you first. Prayer is your receiving and responding. Approached in this way, prayer-as-slow-listening is much easier than if you imagine that it depends on your efforts, your words, your trying to pay attention, and so on.

With Scripture the conversation starts from God. It's like a friend greeting you from across the street. The friend starts the contact: you didn't even notice he or she was there.

Return to that marvellous image of how God looks after us, 'as a mother comforting her child'. It already speaks to you: otherwise you would not have singled it out. If you want to deepen your personal prayer, there is one almost infallible way. Have the courage to linger over a phrase like this. Repeat it to yourself quietly. We can read the words so quickly. But if it is to reach the more deeply, we need to take time. Then gradually the wonder of it can sink in: the image of the mother caring for a child in need of consolation is one of the simplest and yet most powerful in human experience. But here it is about God . . .

Then you mentioned the sequence in Luke 10 that gives us both the parable of the Good Samaritan and the visit of Jesus to Martha and Mary. Your comment on the possible contrast was 'dead on', and I'll come to that in a moment. Parables are meant to jolt us, but the trouble is that we know them too well, or think we do. We can be just like the man who asked Jesus, 'who is my neighbour?': he knew the Law backwards and could recite it off *by* heart, but he didn't know it *in* the heart. The story Jesus told shook him into realizing the meaning of those words he had recited about love. Prayer has the same aim – of moving from surface contact with Christian ideals to letting them become powerful and personal in the presence of Jesus.

So ask Jesus the same dangerous question: who is *your* neighbour? Who needs your care now? And pause to let his story have an impact on you. It comes as a shock to hear how the officially religious people saw but pretended not to see the wounded man, and then this hated outsider turns out to be the hero. Take your time. Ponder what roads you are asked to cross, or what calls you tend to avoid, but don't let it sink into self-blaming for 'not being better to people'. If it's prayer, talk from the heart to the Lord. Let *him* guide you to the concrete courage you need in caring for someone.

On the same Sunday in fact there was another Old Testament passage that comments on this parable. It says that what God wants of you is far from impossible, or distant. Instead 'the word is very near to you, it is in your mouth and in your heart for you to put into practice' (Deuteronomy 30:14). Prayer is the special space where you listen to God's word 'in your heart'. We all usually want to be more caring. But in prayer Christ sets us free from just wishful thinking, and our imagination is liberated to live that love.

You are right to suggest that the episode of Martha and Mary seems to contradict the parable. One says: be active and cross the road to help. The other stresses: sit down and listen and don't fuss in the kitchen. Perhaps

35

they are side by side with a purpose (indeed some Scripture experts would agree with your hunch). The parable is about our dealings with people in need. The conflict in the house of his friends puts the focus on Jesus. Others need us. We need Jesus. There are two loves at the heart of Christianity. One is active, the other passive.

So Martha's mistake was not in her generosity but over the identity of her visitor. Mary saw that in the presence of Jesus another wavelength becomes appropriate, one of quiet receiving rather than of busy serving. To pray a passage like that, some people find it helpful to envisage the scene, even to imagine themselves in the two roles: we all fuss and yet we all have a 'still point', as the poet T. S. Eliot called it. Gradually, the attention can turn to Jesus in the scene, and then little by little we can enter that silence of adoration that is the attitude of Mary.

If those two passages of Luke, side by side, contrast the two loves, here's an image that might help to make the connection between the love we receive from God and the love we give to others. Picture the link between the two loves as being like an upside-down capital T. God comes down to us (the vertical line). We go out to others (the horizontal line). It is really one love, flowing in two ways. And where the two points touch is where prayer happens. Prayer means that soaking in of love embodied by Mary sitting at the feet of Jesus: even that detail about her posture is a beautiful symbol of contemplative listening. But prayer is also a source of active energy flowing into our real worlds: it gives the strength to cross the road and do something.

Have the courage to rest where those two lines meet, where those two loves flow. Scripture, savoured quietly and personally, will change you: the love you receive from the Lord, is the love you learn to share and live in new ways.

Letter 8

PRAYER FROM THE BIBLE

Some time later, Padraig reported on progress: I've gone beyond the mass leaflets you were talking about in your last letter to me. I've actually bought a Bible and even if it's a bit confusing, I'm finding my way around it. It's one of those editions with some introductions to each book and some notes on most pages. Have you any more suggestions for using it to pray?

Dear Padraig,

Yes, the Bible seems a complicated book. Someone has said that it's really a library, a set of many books. I would not advise you to read it from start to finish. For a beginner some parts will be more suitable for meditation. The reading of certain books or passages will nourish your spiritual life more than others.

Obviously the New Testament is the climax of the Bible for a Christian. But it's only about a fifth of the whole book. For personal prayer my guess is that, for the moment, you'll find more fruit in the Gospels and in the Letters. More of that later.

But let's not forget the riches of the Old Testament, even though it can be very 'confusing' as you say. It's written in many different styles – from poetry to legal prescriptions, from parable-tales to religious philosophy, from history to exhortations of the prophets. Gradually you'll find yourself at home with it. To have texts to pray from, I'd be inclined to focus initially on the Psalms and on passages from the prophets.

Before I come to some particular passages or suggestions, let's remember what the Bible is. It's a love story written over many centuries. On one side it is very simple: God wants people to know they are loved and that they can live lives of love. But on our side we 'mess things up' – to put it in modern terms – and so the love story becomes more complex.

God is steady. We are unsteady. The drama of the Bible – perhaps even the drama of life – comes from that difference. You wouldn't need to read books on prayer if you were full of God's steadiness of love. I can write these letters but please don't imagine for a moment that I always live them *steadily*. It's because of my unsteadiness that I need the Bible, to remind my mind and heart of the promise of God. God has big hopes for us. We forget. God's book recalls us to what we are meant to be.

In the Church there is a long and deep history of people reading the Bible prayerfully. But the false impression that this book was not for everyone goes far back: a generation before St Patrick came to Ireland, St John Chrysostom wrote to the laity, 'you think reading the Bible is only for monks but you have even more need of it'. You can put that beside some words of Cardinal Martini, the Archbishop of Milan: 'I am convinced that for a Christian today it is difficult, if not impossible, to keep one's faith without nourishing oneself through listening to Scripture personally as well as with others. In this way a believer learns to rest in the heart of God and one trains oneself to look at people and their weaknesses with the eyes of God'.

Indeed the Second Vatican Council encouraged 'frequent reading' of Scripture for 'all the Christian faithful'. But your question, Padraig, is about *how*. What I want to suggest in this letter draws on an old tradition in the Church. I want to describe what was known for centuries as *lectio divina*, literally divine reading, meaning prayerful reading of Scripture, and then to use this approach on a marvellous text in Isaiah.

First, find chapter 43 (verses 1–5) in the prophet Isaiah. It's a passage that has become well-known in its sung version – 'Be not Afraid'. To begin you simply read the short few verses slowly. Be patient with yourself as you get acquainted with each detail. This first stage involves your eyes, your lips (it can be good to read it aloud quietly) but most of all your mind. As you try to understand these words, you begin to realize how much they are saying – about you being created by God, about you being saved, about you being protected in all dangers, about God being always with you, about God's love.

Already you have moved from reading to pondering. Now little by little you move from reflecting with the mind to receiving with the heart. This is spoken to you. This touches you. The reading becomes relationship. Prayer becomes conversation. With this Isaiah text, you can quietly be overwhelmed with its consoling promise and gift of love. Nearly 1800 years ago St Cyprian gave a beautifully simple description of all this: 'if you give yourself to reading and to prayer, sometimes God will speak with you, and sometimes you with God'.

Reading. Pondering. Conversation. Another stage can be called 'resting'. What started from words now goes

40

beyond words. The poetry of Isaiah leads you into a kind of quiet wonder. It is typical at this moment of *lectio divina* to pause on one phrase, and to enjoy it with gratitude and in inner silence. 'You are precious in my eyes'. You pause and let yourself know the reality of that love-sentence from God.

Finally, some old writers mentioned a fifth stage of 'living' it all. Sometimes in the ordinary tasks of life you can deliberately remember a phrase of the Scripture – like a bee collecting for honey, as was once said. Or more generally you can let the power of this passage change your attitude to people and to events. We all need to forgive, or to be kinder, or to let that love be lived.

Don't get too caught up in the five stages. It's just a description of what happens normally if you give time to praying the Scriptures. But before I end let me mention some other Bible passages that you could 'use' for prayer in this way – texts taken from three different families of biblical writing.

> Psalm 138 (139), which begins 'Lord you know me', can be a great prayer for realizing God's personal love.
>
> Paul's Letter to the Ephesians, 3:14–21, is a powerful prayer for growth in one's inner self.
>
> The scene of the healing of blind Bartimaeus, at the end of Mark 10, can invite you into a similar meeting with the Lord.

Letter 9

OFFENDING GOD?

Jim writes: I have read somewhere that there are four main forms of prayer – prayer of adoration or praise, of thanksgiving, of intercession, and of forgiveness. It's the last I want to hear more about. What does it mean to ask for God's forgiveness? It sounds as if God might be in bad humour and not forgive me, if I don't ask politely. Now that I think of it, how is God really 'offended' by my sins? I admit that I fall into various kinds of selfishness, with boring predictability. But I feel that when I try to pray about this area of my life, I regress to being a schoolboy in trouble with the headmaster, waiting outside his door, and wondering what is in store for me. I'm convinced there is something I am missing in all this. How should I pray about sin and forgiveness?

Dear Jim,

You've put your finger on something vital. Perhaps there is no topic in Christian life that risks remaining so shadowed by memories from childhood. The field of sin and forgiveness, as you suggest, is deeply connected with images of God. So I'd like to spend a little time clearing the ground before I come to your main question – how to pray this whole area.

Take your vivid picture of yourself outside the headmaster's office. It's accurate, I fear, for how many people think of sin and pardon. But that image is all wrong about sin, and about God's forgiveness. You are right: what we learned as children about sin has stayed with us, and may not have matured much. A small child can only understand sin in terms of breaking a law, or displeasing an authority figure, or just of being caught and punished. If the child is told that 'God is merciful', that is taken to mean that God will not be too severe with me, if I admit my bad behaviour. I will get off lightly, provided I don't do it again. The headmaster is in good humour today! This whole model is immature, but it lingers in the background of most of us adults, and it needs a real effort to replace it with something more worthy.

Where to begin? I have written elsewhere about St Peter's discovery of a genuine sense of sin (*Where is Your God?* in the chapter on prayer). Just remember the key moment in Luke 5, where Peter falls before Jesus with the cry, 'Leave me, Lord; I am a sinful man'. It is crucial, I think, to notice that this sense of unworthiness happens when Peter has just had the greatest catch of fish in his whole life. When surrounded by the wonder of the gift, he knows *by contrast* his own mediocrity of response. Glimpsing the love of the Giver, he sees his own life as missing or resisting a *relationship*.

There is an important light here for discovering a mature sense of sin. You won't get it from reading these pages. You won't get it from delving even honestly into the egoisms of your life. On your own, you can arrive at a sense of wrong or of evil. But a real sense of sin is received only in the presence of Christ, like Peter found. It is born in that flow of friendship with the Lord; otherwise it remains on the level of a lonely sense of failure.

That is the difference between guilt and sorrow. Guilt is a merely negative self-blaming. But sorrow is a liberating grace, born from looking into the eyes of the Lord. Within that relationship, like Peter overwhelmed with gratitude, I can see my sin as something out of tune with all I have been given. With that encounter I learn from the eyes of the Lord, so to speak, that I am loved in my very weakness.

The truth about sin and forgiveness is profoundly relational and you enter that relationship especially through prayer. In that spirit of prayer you can best realize the healing love which means forgiveness. (And this emphasis on relationship and prayer is equally relevant for Catholics in celebrating the sacrament of reconciliation: that most human of sacraments needs something of this spiritual tone, if it is not to fall into ritualism.)

Jim, all that is an attempt to answer your cluster of questions. It is through a certain level of personal prayer that you can get rid of that headmaster sense of God and arrive at a genuine awareness of both sin and forgiveness. Start from gratitude – like St Peter's experience of wonder faced with those overflowing nets. It is there that you begin to glimpse who you are meant to be and *then* how you fall short of the love you could live. Even if there are painful failures to be confronted, do so in prayer, in relationship. From all this a different sense of sin can come to life, not on the child's level of law-infringement, or displeasing the parents, but starting from the wholeness God invited you into.

Indeed, in the Greek of the Gospels the word for sin is *hamartia*, which comes from archery and means 'missing the mark'. I find that image much more helpful than the childhood echoes of 'sin'. It suggests that there is a

goal for my heart, but the arrow of my real living falls
short. Sin is this forgetting of who I am meant to be and
of Who has huge hopes for me. It resists the fullness of
humanity that I am invited towards. It avoids the pain
of being truly free. It is a stunting of my growth towards
loving more like Christ. Sorrow therefore is an awakening (like Peter's) that comes only in the presence of the
Lord. It involves a new reading of my reality through
his eyes.

Ignatius Loyola, among many others, suggests that
this grace of sorrow is best found by meditating on
Christ crucified: 'imagine Christ our Lord present before
you upon the cross, begin to speak with him ... exactly
as one friend speaks to another'. In this respect I greatly
value the insight of Sebastian Moore that on the Cross I
see the person I do not dare to be. I see the One who is
Love, being murdered by unlove. Placing myself there,
I realize a deep face of sin: it is how I crucify love in my
own life. So the crucifix becomes the mirror of how I
suppress fullness of life in myself and others. In coward-
ice or laziness, I have preferred half-life. I am the crucifier
of true life in me.

And, in the same prayer-moment, I can see God's
'forgiveness' as embracing all this self-wounding called
sin. Forgiveness is not like the headmaster being surprisingly lenient. Indeed the human analogies are all a little
lacking. When I ask someone to forgive me, and
especially if that person has been offended by me, I'm
really asking him or her to stop holding that fault against
me, to drop the coldness, to renew the friendship. But
this cannot be true of God. God does not carry grudges
or avoid speaking to me. To ask God to forgive is not
seeking a change of God's mood, some softening of
harshness. God's forgiveness does not mean a change in

45

God but in me. It is God's never-withdrawn love reaching where I have withdrawn some part of me from that love. Forgiveness means receiving healing for that self-hurt.

So forgiveness changes me, and it does so, paradoxically, when I realize prayerfully that God's love has never changed. Or rather, it only changes its tone so as to reach where I am refusing. Forgiveness is the name for God's love when it touches our sin, our closedness, our hurt. A parent loves a child but that love expresses itself differently when the child is sick. It is the same love but a different need. Forgiveness is like that.

To quote Sebastian Moore again, 'to *see* sin is to see its forgiveness' which means 'the unhardening of the heart' – not God's heart but mine. Forgiveness does not mean that God now relents and relates to me again. Forgiveness is the quality God's love takes on, as it touches the heart that *I* have hardened into stone. Such forgiveness, when I let it reach me, unfreezes my fear and releases the flow of goodness again. I come to know that I am a loved sinner. In fact for God there are no unloved sinners.

We have come a long way from being in trouble with the headmaster. In the light of all this it is relatively easy to answer your question about offending God. That expression has a traditional place in prayers many of us learned as children, but what picture does it conjure up? It can be a misleading way of expressing a real truth: it can even give the idea of God going into a sulk. By sin we offend against life, against love, against ourselves, against others. Yes, we 'offend' God, but only because God identifies with life, with love, with ourselves, with others. 'As often as you did it to one of these, you did it to me' (Matthew 25:40).

As far as praying about sin, what has been said already

can be summed up like this: start from gratitude, not from self-blame; make it a prayer of relationship with Christ crucified; then sorrow and forgiveness are liberating graces, even though with a background of pain. To finish, let me make two suggestions of Gospel passages to help you pray this experience of sin and forgiveness.

Look at the powerful scene in Luke 7, the contrast between the woman and the Pharisee (vv. 36–50). She is in touch with her vulnerability, and he is unable to emerge from behind his shields. Who is the sinner? Who has the heart of flesh and who the heart of stone? (Look up Ezekiel 36:26.)

Remember the parable of the prodigal son (Luke 15:11–32). It has, in a sense, four journeys. A journey away. A coming to oneself. A return journey. And most important of all: the running of the Father to welcome his son home. At its core is the pigsty moment, when he 'hits rock bottom' as we say today, but when the memory of home makes him realize he does not have to continue like this. Notice too the little drama of the elder brother. Commentators have been hard on him. Yes, he is another face of sin, closed like Simon the Pharisee. But his tragedy is that he is happy and does not know it: 'you are with me always'.

As usual, let such passages become personal through prayer. Do not be content to think of them as about other people. They are about you, and about the forgiveness of an 'unoffended' God.

Letter 10

TRAGEDY AND UNANSWERED PRAYERS

Anne writes: I have a simple question about prayer. I wonder whether I should bother the Lord with my needs! Does God really answer our prayers? Perhaps I should tell you that a good deal of agony and agonizing lies behind this question. Last year I had to watch a good friend dying of cancer at the age of 44. We were in school together, and we always kept up contact. Like me, Sharon was a mother of three children, the eldest now 17. Sharon had a good deal of silent faith but I don't know if she ever really prayed to be cured. But I prayed that God would spare her life. But the illness just took its course and killed her slowly. Now I wonder if there was any point at all in my prayer?

Dear Anne,

That was not easy to face. Perhaps not easy to write either. I have no quick answers. Indeed I would much prefer to meet you than to respond on paper. But with all those reservations, here goes. Perhaps most deathbeds are scenes of unanswered prayer. Or better, of *seemingly* unanswered prayer.

If we take an easier and less painful example, it might

help to shed light on your question. Imagine someone praying for good weather for a wedding day and let's suppose in fact that it pours with rain. Has their prayer gone unanswered? On the surface, yes. But what was the real desire behind that prayer? Is not the good weather a part of wanting the wedding day to 'go well'? And is not that in turn a part of praying that the whole life of marriage will be blessed and good? Nobody seriously believes that a rainy wedding day will cause an unhappy marriage.

Do you see what I'm getting at? If our smaller petitions remain seemingly unanswered, we trust that God is surely answering the bigger desires behind them. We do not know this at the time. Often it is only *afterwards* that we can begin to understand – rather like those two depressed disciples walking away from Jerusalem after the horror of the crucifixion of their master. They were shattered and disillusioned. 'We had hoped . . .' they say. But . . .

In that great scene (at the end of Luke's Gospel) the Risen Lord himself acts as consoler. He gives them a different light on suffering. Slowly they emerge from shock and glimpse a pattern behind the outer tragedy that has left them so broken. Now walking with the Lord (which is prayer) their hearts listen and even 'burn' with the wonder of what they are coming to realize.

The Gospel does not tell us what parts of Scripture Jesus 'opened' to them. Possibly he touched on the famous 'Servant Songs' in Isaiah. Those deep poems explore how what seems futility can become fruitful in God's own way. 'While I was thinking, . . . "I have exhausted myself for nothing", all the while my cause was with the Lord' (49:4). 'We thought of him as someone . . . struck by God; yet . . . through his wounds

49

we are healed' (53:4–5). Notice that in both those sentences there is a contrast between the way we think and the way God sees things. Where we can see only grief or tragedy, God can in time bring about newness of life.

But to move from numbness to serenity takes prayer and (especially in a situation of mourning) a lot of time. While waiting for that slow peace, there is no reason to feel guilty if you seem confused over things, or even angry with God in a sense. The Psalms are full of such feelings. So if you give honest expression to them in prayer, you are in a great tradition.

In fact you are in the tradition of Jesus himself in the Garden of Gethsemane. His was also a prayer of struggle, of fear, and of confusion before death, which is marvellously consoling for us. In Matthew's Gospel twice he prays with a negative: 'My Father, if this cup *cannot* pass by, but I must drink it, your will be done!' (26:42). This is far from a pagan resignation to fate. His was a prayer of relationship, of trust and tenderness, however, dark and agonized. In one sense his prayer was not answered, and in a deeper sense, yes it was. He asked for life, and he was raised into Life, and at the centre of that journey was an obedient trust in the Father even through the horror of Good Friday. Remember the numbness of his cry 'My God, my God, why have you forsaken me?' (from Psalm 22). Do not hesitate to join in that cry – of both agony and dark faith – when you think of Sharon.

Someone has counted and found that Jesus calls God 'Father' or 'Abba' (like Daddy) 170 times in the Gospels. His many prayers reach out to the Father with confidence – no matter what the situation. Even while weeping at the tomb of Lazarus, his prayer begins: 'Father, I know that you always hear me' (John 11:42). Your prayer can start from the same surrender and the same struggling trust, and especially so in times of weeping and agony.

In everything to do with prayer, we have our best model in Jesus himself. It is he who tells us both to ask for what we need, and that the Father knows our needs before we ask (Matthew 6:9; 7:7). Whether we are praying for good weather for the wedding, or pleading for the life of a sick friend, our prayers don't express something unknown to God. They don't try to bridge a gap between us and a God who is distant. God already knows. God is already with us in our desires. Our prayers are not like 'making a wish' in the direction of God. All prayer involves some reaching out with childlike trust, even when the inner tone is chaotic or full of confusion. Prayer is always more than petition, even if petition is always a strand in prayer. Even if you do not use his words, all praying echoes the surrender of Jesus: not my will but yours. We ask for what we think is best, but we try to hand everything over to the One who knows even better.

If prayer does not have a little of this relationship of deep trust, there is a danger that a magical image of God can be lurking unnoticed. Do you remember how God was shown in some old films – pointing a finger and 'zap', some strange event takes place? I think of the crossing of the Red Sea as presented by the famous Cecil B. de Mille. Our Christian God is much more mysterious than that. Those childish images do small justice to the God of Jesus Christ, who did not 'answer' the Son's prayer in the garden of agony. There was no easy 'zap'. But there was the Resurrection after the darkness. And that is the ground of all our hoping, especially when faced with the stark shock of death. How well I remember rushing to that hospital room – after a midnight phone call – and finding my mother so visibly 'gone'. First thoughts are not of resurrection, but last ones are.

Perhaps it's when such shadows come that we learn a different wavelength of prayer. The seeming silence and absence of God is an invitation to let the net down into deeper waters (Luke 5:4). This is not an easy journey, but it touches so many deep things of the heart and of hope.

Letter 11

WHEN IS PRAYER GENUINE?

Pauline writes: I am a religious, and so I have had some 'training' in prayer over the years. But recently I have a new doubt about it all. I wonder what I'm really doing when I pray. I'm afraid I can just use it to feel comfortable in myself. Could it all be selfish instead of spiritual? Or in fact spiritually selfish? How can I know if my prayer is genuine? I'll add that I've occasionally noticed that when prayer 'goes well', I end up pleased with myself, and afterwards I can easily be rough in my judgement on others or unkind in various ways. Surely this is a bad sign. I then begin to question the whole thing as having any Christian fruit.

Dear Pauline,
You are asking probing questions there, and they have to be asked. They echo those Gospel passages where Jesus made fun of false prayer. Don't forget that his descriptions of pious pride were often comic, but we are so used to them that we can miss it. Think of the parable of the Pharisee and the publican (in Luke 18) or the description of the person who always prays 'Lord, Lord' but does nothing about it (Matthew 7:21–7), or again of

the picture of people praying at street corners so that everyone will notice them (Matthew 6:5–6). Any good story-teller would have his audience laughing at such material, simply by fleshing it out a bit. The Gospel gives us the skeleton plot, not the full ironic performance of Jesus!

All of these satires of his show that prayer can easily fail to be 'genuine' as you put it, and that it becomes a sham mainly when we turn in on ourselves and do not enlarge our lives into love. Exactly these two false notes are present in the Pharisee of the parable: he talks mainly about himself, about the great things he is doing – with a certain self-satisfaction and conceit. But he reveals his falsity more by looking down his spiritual nose at people who fall into obvious sins like adultery or corruption.

Which of us, even in church, has not occasionally judged someone else externally, just like the Pharisee does to the publican at the back of the temple? And criticizing someone else is often an indirect way of shielding myself from much the same criticism. When I worship at the altar of my own goodness, I am not really reaching out to God, and when I find myself sitting with the judge's wig on and being harsh on others, even in prayer, there is certainly something wrong. I need to move to the very different attitude of the publican: he recognizes his own need to change and he looks to God to convert his heart and life. He does not begin every sentence with 'I' as the Pharisee does.

So am I agreeing with your own self-doubt: perhaps your prayer could 'all be selfish'? Firstly, watch that word 'all'! I think you have latched on to a sensitive danger for anyone who tries to pray – a kind of creeping self-satisfaction and pride. *But* don't fall into the trap of throwing out the baby with the bath water, of dismissing

54

the many good desires and fruits of your prayer simply because *sometimes* you catch yourself being 'spiritually selfish'. When that happens, the call is to recognize it honestly, and to come back humbly – like that publican. Beware of doubting the whole business of your prayer just because you occasionally find traces of Narcissism.

Negative Magnifying Glass

Let me share with you my favourite image about how we can be deceived – in prayer or in other areas. I should admit that I've used it before but not in these letters (it appeared in a book called *Where Is Your God?*). But I have found that it has given surprising help to people and so I don't hesitate to 'use' it again.

I have a theory (to be taken with a grain of salt) that the devil has a factory that specializes in manufacturing one object only: negative magnifying glasses! Think of holding a magnifying glass over this page. Some words will become HUGE, but the rest of the page will be distorted and you won't be able to read it all.

Besides, since it is a *negative* magnifying glass, it will pick out all the failures and dark areas and highlight them. If so, the real damage comes from not being able to read the rest of the page of your experience – the good fruit of prayer, the times when it nourished your heart and your commitment to living with love. In your case, you are right to notice when something good like prayer gets twisted into something self-serving or egoistic. But don't let that occasional fall prevent you from trusting that your desire to try to pray is itself good and usually, to use your words, 'genuine' in its fruits.

Yardstick of Love

You spoke of judging prayer by its 'Christian fruit'. In that light how can we recognize the fruits of authentic Christian prayer? Both St Peter and St Paul offer fascinating lists in their letters and if we put them together, we have a way of measuring when the Spirit is working in our lives and in our prayer. In his Letter to the Galatians (chapter 5) Paul mentions many kinds of self-indulgence and then adds: 'What the Spirit brings is very different: love, joy, peace, patience, kindness, goodness, trustfulness, gentleness and self-control.' They are goals and gifts and ways of measuring our lives: but don't worry, nobody lives all of them perfectly all of the time.

When St Peter offers his list (at the beginning of his second letter), he seems to have a kind of ladder in mind with various rungs. Faith leads to goodness, and that leads on to understanding, then to self-control, to patience, to genuine prayerfulness, to kindness to all, and finally 'love' as a crown of everything.

Isn't it interesting that Paul begins with love and Peter ends with it? And I notice at least four other qualities that both of them mention (work them out for yourself). But of course the test of love is *the* Christian yardstick, indeed the one given by Jesus himself at the Last Supper just after speaking of his 'new commandment': 'in this way all will know you as my disciples' (John 13: 34–5).

I remember talking to a student once who said that all of Christianity is summed up in loving one another. I answered, a little to his surprise, 'yes, but finish the sentence'. The ending makes all the difference: 'as I have loved you' (John 15:12). Christian loving is not just a nice warm feeling, which on its own is not likely to survive the tough moments of life. The love we are talking about is concrete, and costly, and above all our way of echoing Christ himself. Without prayer such love is next to impossible because the new commandment of Jesus is not a new external law. Nor does the second half of the sentence mean that he is just a model to be imitated. It goes deeper than that.

His new commandment is a gift. It is a new power he offers us, of sharing his own attitudes, or in a bad but memorable pun, his be-attitudes. As a mystic of centuries ago put it, when you watch Christ attentively with the heart, you become like him almost without knowing it: 'love arrives at likeness'. That is William of St Thierry, a Cistercian of the twelfth century.

I said just now that love is *the* yardstick for prayer. Yes, but that love – 'as I have loved you' – included the self-giving of the Cross. Although we are never asked to seek out the cross, our love, learned from him, will be able to carry the cross with him, whenever it comes.

Then prayer will surely be genuine – because it's impossible to fake that costly self-giving. There is a marvellous expression of this certainty in St John's letter. Speaking of how we share the journey with Christ, he says that 'we have passed out of death and into life, and of this we can be *sure* because we love' (1 John 3:14). That sentence is revolutionary in its view of Christian truth: we know, not by working it out in thought, but by living it out in the everyday passover called love. *That* is the real test against the Pharisee in us all.

To glimpse that love in Christ is the goal of prayer. To echo that love with Christ is what you call Christian fruit of an infallible kind.

Letter 12

CHRISTMAS
AND CONTEMPLATION

Pauline writes back: I liked the quotation from William of St Thierry that when we look at Christ in the silence of the heart we can come to resemble him slowly. I've never heard of that particular writer and I'm sure that there are countless other old authors of depth and wisdom that I know nothing about. You talked about the 'contemplative tradition', and I suppose it was mainly a matter of enclosed monks and sisters. But surely they have something that can be translated into our more complex culture and for active religious like me. I've some sense of what it means to let simpler prayer happen, but I need nourishment. As they used to say in examination papers, please comment!

Dear Pauline,
Your letter comes just in time for me to reply before Christmas and indeed what I want to say can fit in well to this season, as I hope you'll see. I could not agree more. To appreciate something of the rich history of contemplative prayer in the Church can make a huge difference for spiritual life today: indeed I'm sure that many people, who are faithful to some personal prayer,

would be greatly helped if they let 'simpler prayer' happen – to use your own expression. The courage to simplify is at the core of that long tradition of the contemplatives.

You don't have to be an enclosed contemplative to do this. Nor do you have to be in the twelfth century! I like this recent story of an Australian mother who went on retreat. She listened to the talks of the retreat director and tried to follow his advice about praying. He suggested thinking about the words of the Our Father phrase by phrase or taking one of the Psalms slowly. It seemed terribly easy but she could not settle into it. After a day of confusion she went to see the director. At one point he asked her: 'If you came on a retreat like this, I'm sure you've tried to pray before, haven't you?' Her reply surprised and delighted him: 'I never try to pray. But every day I sit some time with God. When I finish, I feel different. It's as if I have been held.'

The retreat director was able to recognize that his methods were downright unhelpful for a woman who naturally had found another wavelength of being with God. Words and thoughts were no use to her. She had gradually arrived at her own way of being present. Indeed what she said is exactly parallel, in its modern language, to what old William was saying. His 'becoming like Christ' was happening in her 'feeling different', just as what she describes as being 'held' is close to what some mystics call 'union' with God. Our Australian friend may never have heard of Hildegard of Bingen, a contemporary of William's in fact, who spoke of 'the embrace of God's *maternal* love'. The language is different but the experience of prayer as resting with God is very similar.

All this means trusting an unfamiliar wavelength. It

can be a confusing transition at first and may seem like 'not praying at all'. St John of the Cross, with his typical down-to-earthness, says that people changing over from active to passive prayer may fear that 'they are doing nothing and wasting time': but, he says, they usually need 'freedom of spirit' to enter this deeper kind of praying.

How would you know if this sort of prayer is right for you? In other words, that God is inviting you to a different level of listening and presence? One sign is that your old way of praying with words and 'holy thoughts' comes to seem dry and empty to you. This *can*, of course, come from your own carelessness (but you would know that easily). Is there a desire for God present? If so, and if you are trying to live a generous Christian life, this may well be the moment to simplify your listening, to let go of too much activity, to create a different silence, and so to be ready for the gift of God's love beyond thoughts or words – like that Australian woman.

'Taste and see that the Lord is good' is a line in Psalm 34 and many of the great mystics had a sense of 'relishing' God: it sums up their experience of how God's gift meets their attentiveness. In this light consider the painting of the old Wise Man tenderly touching the foot of Jesus and seeming to rest his head on the knee of Mary (it comes from the monastery of Subiaco in central Italy and is reproduced opposite). It is a perfect example of this meeting of gift and attention. The infant Jesus has one hand on the head of the old man and with the other is blessing him. There is no sense of effort or struggle, just of quiet belonging. You could spend time just gazing at that picture, and finding there an invitation to let go of too many words or thoughts in prayer.

The Magi or Wise Men had come on a long journey

60

61

to arrive at this climax of discovery. The star did not stay steady for them. When it disappeared, they ran into danger by asking the wrong person the way – Herod who seemed so welcoming but wanted to kill. But they kept going even in the dark, stayed together and brought their gifts. It's a marvellous image for any of us on the Christian road: coping with darkness, persevering in hard times, being with one another, and trying to give of ourselves. But here in this picture of contemplation is the core of our life, the encounter with Christ. There is darkness and struggle in the story but this picture is of gentleness and peace. It reminds me of a modern summary of contemplative prayer as 'silence that is presence and presence that is silence'.

Should you then abandon your old forms of prayer? Not necessarily. But have the imagination to recognize when it is right to move on to something simpler. Sometimes a person can keep an anchor in words or images. You could take a line of Scripture or even this painting as a starting-point. But then allow yourself to enter a zone of slow conversation leading to inner quiet. If distractions come, return to your anchor, and then launch out again into those deeper waters of silence and presence.

Inevitably this letter has oversimplified contemplative prayer. There is so much more to it, including deep dyings to self in darkness. This grace of quiet prayer can be gritty and tough at times: we have to be weaned from superficial desires even for God's consolation. But my main hope here has been to encourage you not to be afraid of crossing new thresholds of silence, because, as life goes on, prayer can and should find a different stillness.

For some people it becomes this remembering of God

with the heart – realizing the love that comes to us in Christ, a love that asks to flow through us into this wounded world. The old man in the painting seems to be relaxing in the river of that love. Why not put yourself there with him?

There is a danger that all this spiritual language can seem off-putting. I'm convinced that with a bit of encouragement most Christians who give some regular time to prayer can reach levels of silent presence with God that at first would not have been possible. I end with a description of prayer which arrived to me from a young man of nineteen whom I know as someone full of energy. But he also has discovered a quiet side and tells us about it very much in his own down-to-earth way.

'I feel closer to God since I started my own form of prayer (which I feel proud of). What I do is, when I go up to bed at night, I turn out the light, pull back the curtains, sit up and gaze at the stars. I usually say a few Our Fathers and Hail Marys to break the ice so to speak. Then I just sit there and pray about the day's events, my ambitions, my hopes and my worries. And sometimes I just sit there and gaze while my mind winds down with the comfort of being in the company of God and his servants. Amazingly this is the highlight of the evening: this is where I feel most at home. It's just the Lord and me and the vast universe in harmony and it is so tranquil and stimulating that if I don't perform my prayer this way I feel as if I've lost something that I can't recapture. Absurd, isn't it? Or is it? I don't know.'

Letter 13

DOES PRAYER NEED TO CHANGE?

David writes: I've always 'said my prayers' and yet I often wonder whether I've missed something. Should I have developed more? I suppose I have learned to rest a bit more with the Lord, not always to splatter him with words. But I have no plan and perhaps I haven't grown as much as I could. Does my prayer need to change? Are there any maps to the change that should happen?

Dear David,

I bet many people will echo what you say there. It's amazing how high the statistics are for people who pray every day in some way: 77 per cent of British Catholics, 83 per cent of Irish Catholics, 85 per cent of American Catholics, and indeed 57 per cent of all Americans in 1989 (as against 53 per cent some fifteen years earlier). And before I leave statistics, one fascinating fact emerges – that of those who are uncertain about the existence of God or reject it, 17 per cent say that they pray every day and 35 per cent once a week!

It's great that so many people keep going in prayer: it would be even better if they could keep growing as well.

So, the brief answer to your question is certainly 'yes': I think it has to be said loud and clear that we are made by God for change. There is a famous statement of Cardinal Newman that 'to live is to change and to have lived fully is to have changed often'.

In this light think about that parable of Jesus about the little seed which slowly becomes a tree and is able to give shelter to the birds of the air. I've always liked that last image. It sums up what we are here for – not just to grow for ourselves but to be able to offer space to others.

Put that side by side with its opposite in the parable of the talents. In this story one man feels so inadequate and 'afraid' that he buries his only gift in the ground. The story pictures God as wanting us to develop our freedom and even as angry at that person's opting for a 'safety first' policy of no risk and no growth. (You'll find those parables in Matthew's Gospel, chapters 13 and 25.) Or take St Paul: he often insists that we are 'not to be childish', that we should get beyond baby food in faith, that we should move on towards maturity in Christ. (See for instance 1 Corinthians 3:2; 14:20.)

Stages of Change

You asked about maps. Some psychologists of faith development have done excellent research in recent decades. Here I want to adapt some insights from one of them, James Fowler, with whom I've had the pleasure of working now and then.

What are the typical changes that we can expect in the journey of faith? I would single out four possible developments, connected with new possibilities that open for us at different stages of life. Most of us start by inheriting our faith as a passive *belonging* through our family to the Church. This is the normal situation for a child – and so we learned to 'say our prayers' as a custom. But once we move on from childhood, that level of faith and of prayer is seldom enough. It's not a matter of abandoning it, but rather of 'enlarging the tent' (a phrase from Isaiah 54:2).

Beyond childhood, the young adult has different needs – especially to experience faith as a *relationship* to Christ. It's a friendship that leads to a choice to live his way. At this time of life prayer can become more personal, nourished by knowing the Jesus of the Gospels. The Letter to the Hebrews has a marvellous piece of advice: keep your eyes on Jesus who leads us in our faith (12:2). Such 'watching' with the eyes of faith is a very important phase in prayer, perhaps especially in early adulthood. And it is not just a fantasy exercise, because the impact of Jesus does not remain locked in the distant past. Prayer always means some present tense encounter. It leads first to intimacy and then to decision or conversion – just as in so many Gospel meetings with Jesus. Indeed all those encounters can be rewritten in the present tense for us – if we allow them prayerfully to sink into the heart.

Later, in so-called middle life, unexpected and *darker shadows* often arrive: people feel tired and nothing seems as simple as we once imagined. The old clarities are not so clear any more. Fatigue is more frequent. Confusion comes down, like that cloud in the scene of the transfiguration that made the disciples afraid (Luke 9:34). Or again, it's like the stage in the Gospels when the apostles were shocked by hearing Jesus speak so much about his dying; they had many struggles within themselves before they accepted what the Kingdom really meant. So, in these middle years of life, prayer may have a touch of agony and of Gethsemane, but more positively it can become more at home with quiet, and can let go of older hopes of controlling everything including oneself. One writer calls this a 'sacrament of self-disappointment', which can lead to more compassion for human suffering and a wise and deep concern for the huge injustices of the world. You can enter those bigger struggles, because you have grappled humbly with your own smaller ones. This time of shadows can bear surprising fruit after what seems like painful pruning.

Finally, in later life, a different *wisdom* often becomes possible. I've noticed how, in comparison with parents, grandparents seem much less anxious about their grandchildren. In God's providence old age can bring another expansion of the heart. In spite of new weakness and burdens (or even because of them), the self becomes less central and prayer relaxes into a gentle trust in God, 'without many words' as the Gospel says. Some old people find that the borderline between prayer and nonprayer fades and that they have a new sense of God, even in the ordinary flow of life. After all the struggles, walking gently with God seems natural and – as they say in the East – like a flowing river drawn by the ocean. One is getting ready to let go at the end into Love – by learning to share God's love already. The Source and Purpose of all our praying and living can become more transparent in old age. We realize – beyond explanations or words – that it is God who is doing the loving, even through the new weakness of our own resources. It can therefore be a time of new serenity in the long adventure of faith.

But David, I hope you are reading all this with a sense of gratitude rather than of guilt. My four stages are too neat but they suggest how faith and prayer may unfold for people. Perhaps you can recognize something of your own journey there, even if you were not conscious of it at the time.

Of course there are more invitations to grow than we usually grasp. We can live below our best and below God's hopes – in prayer and in other ways. But don't underestimate what you mentioned in passing – that you have learned to rest with God in prayer. That's marvellous. You now have the courage to let go of words that 'splatter' the Lord – I like that word of yours – and so you can be there in inner quiet, with what St John of the Cross calls 'loving attentiveness'.

In general life invites us to more simplicity in prayer. Because of fear or routine we can remain 'stuck' in a form of praying that *was* suitable once but doesn't really suit any more. Don't get me wrong: I'm not suggesting you give up saying 'vocal' prayers. But make sure you say them in a way that allows a quieter sense of God to develop. With something like the rosary the words can become background music for the heart that watches the 'mystery'.

As well as this, don't be afraid to pray without set forms. You mention having no plan: even reading about prayer can encourage you to try out some different approaches. Above all use Scripture as a starting-point and anchor, and then have the courage to listen to God in silence.

Yes, over the years our sense of God changes. I like the story of a friend of mine who approached a hermit for advice on prayer, expecting to hear much wisdom. He only got four words from the holy man: 'pray in, not up'. And he went away with this a bit disappointed, until he discovered that they contained a nugget of gold. It makes a world of difference to realize that God is not only beyond us but, as Jesus said of the Spirit: 'with you and within you' (John 14:17).

Letter 14

CROSSING THE DESERT
OF DULLNESS

John writes: Sometimes prayer is simply impossible. I would like to be attentive, deep, listening, consoled, and to feel that fruit is coming from this encounter with the Lord. But the demon of dullness takes over. I am just heavy, stranded, exhausted, and worse, with little desire or energy to do anything about it.

In this light, why is it important to give time to prayer? Particularly when I'm tired inside, long prayer seems a waste of effort, and I mean tired inside myself more than just physically exhausted. Why not be content then with a few minutes? I thought Jesus told us not to make long prayers?

Dear John,
Your last question is the easiest to answer: what Jesus was criticizing was long and showy prayers using 'many words'. I can still remember some of them from my childhood, full of elaborate phrases as if God would be impressed with our eloquence. But the key answer from Jesus comes from his own practice of praying at length, often at night on the mountain.

Your larger question is much harder to deal with. You

describe being 'tired inside'. It's a real experience. In my different way I think I know what you are talking about. It sometimes happens that as soon as I begin a time of prayer, I run into some opposition with myself: churned up feelings about some event of the day, some worry over something yet to come, or just inner fatigue. Especially when the going is uphill in this way, I need time 'to cross the barren desert'.

This phrase, as I'm sure you know, comes from Isaiah 43 (popular in a musical version as 'Be not Afraid'), and it promises that even in times of parching dryness, the Spirit is at work and so there is no danger of 'dying of thirst'. The image fits perfectly with occasions when you find yourself 'stranded', without even the desire to do much about it. It is a sort of spiritual sluggishness, drained of energy. You have come to try to pray but somehow you never find the initial focus or reverence. You are there physically but the heart seems absent and uninterested. Even when you try to anchor yourself in some words of Scripture, it doesn't hold you for more than a few seconds.

How to cross this barren desert? For me the answer lies in a special kind of patience. You need courage to wait through the dreary stage of self-fatigue and then perhaps to embrace a deeper silence of trusting. The next time this 'drooping' mood strikes, try something like this. First of all, notice and admit to yourself the low spirits you find yourself in. Stay with that emptiness and dull pain, but before the Lord. Remember the words of Jesus: come to me all you who are burdened and I will refresh you.

As you admit that burdened sense of self, you might even realize its source. Something has left you disappointed or hurt. If so, bring that to the Lord. But even if nothing specific turns up, it can help simply to give time to this humble honesty: it's an 'off' day for you, but it is the only starting-point you have. You have to start the journey of prayer-listening from where you are. Pretending that you are in great shape will do no good.

It's often a question of time, of waiting. You may be surprised how your heart changes after, say, twenty minutes of sheer tussle and wanting to run away. If you hold your situation up to the Lord, if you trust in spite of darkness, often you will be carried across that barren desert in ways that cannot be explained. Not that your outer situation will be different afterwards, but the horizon of your heart can alter – from stone to flesh, from confused to courageous even if still a little numb.

Let me put it personally. I am amazed at how easy it is to receive that 'refreshment' that Jesus promises, *if* I myself can endure long enough to find again the anchor of my hunger. Smothered underneath my dullness is a quiet zone of hope and trust. But to reach it is like wading through fog until there is better visibility. In the words of Meister Eckhart, 'sit still, and do not waver from your emptiness'!

On a more common-sense level, it's like many a human situation. Have you never been disappointed with yourself over some meeting with a friend? Perhaps especially having built up your hopes for some special occasion, when the moment comes something goes wrong or you are simply not in the best of form. It can be a bit like that in the relationship of prayer, with the big difference that God is a different kind of friend, who will never blame you for what you cannot help, a friend who knows you through and through.

So it's not God who is the problem. It's yourself you have to cope with on those dull days of no focus and no feeling. I have no infallible formula that will ease that pain. But, as I've been suggesting, some dos and don'ts might help. Don't try what is impossible. Don't blame yourself for how you are. Do face reality *humbly* and be patient with some small step forward in prayerfulness.

Obviously you need a certain courage not to abandon the effort when these 'demons' of dullness take over. But I have one concrete suggestion for dealing with these difficult days. It may seem strange but it might work. I have been saying: make this numbness the starting-point of your prayer. I think it can help to express this aloud. Not too loud of course. But if you have a room to yourself, you can at least voice some of your situation and feeling of helplessness not just in silence. It is surprising how the sound of your own voice can gather the scattered self – speaking slowly, with pauses of silence, honestly and simply speaking words from the heart. From this telling of your truth to the Lord, a grace of freedom can come. The voice becomes an anchor for your wandering attention. Your direct speaking of your difficulties and desires can be a very genuine prayer. It's as if you are creating a little psalm of quiet desolation in your own words. And remember, of course, how often the psalms voice moments of confusion and emptiness directly to the Lord.

If making your own psalm of protest or pain seems impossible, at least you can 'retreat' to some slow vocal prayers, and again say the words slowly – quietly but aloud. You could take one of the psalms I mentioned, or the Our Father (but very slowly). And try the method of saying it quietly but aloud.

Don't get me wrong. This 'technique' is nothing more than a way of preparing yourself to be more ready for grace. The Lord answers your desire in ways we cannot foresee. Sometimes, yes, it will be within the time of prayer, and can take the form of a felt change of mood, a lifting of your spirit, a sense of presence and love from God. But that change in mood or feeling is not essential. It may come. It may not.

Remember that the real fruit of prayer is not in some intense feeling, nor in some 'successful' sense of being present. In theory that's easy. In practice it's hard to accept fully. It's right to enjoy the pleasures of prayer when they are available, and when they do not become self-satisfaction. But those 'good times' are not always good for us, and certainly not the real measure of prayer. In those tougher times we are forced to weigh the whole thing differently. The key or yardstick is whether my heart is learning to love, not only by feeling at peace with the Lord (even peace can be lazy or deceptive), but in the infallible test of ordinary life. And surprisingly some of those empty days can produce even more fruit. Just as during some of the painful times of life, we grow in wisdom or compassion perhaps more than when everything goes smoothly – even though we often do not know it until well afterwards. It is possible to view it all in the light of the words of Jesus to Peter at the washing of the feet: 'At the moment you do not know what I am doing, but later you will understand' (John 13:7).

Letter 15

QUESTIONS ABOUT NEW AGE

I have several friends, writes Susan, who were born into the Church but are now involved in spiritual movements of another kind. Recently I have become interested myself in what they are discovering, and I find it very attractive. I went on a weekend of New Age meditation, or expansion-of-awareness, as they call it. It certainly met some of my spiritual needs in a way that the usual Church menu never did. For instance, a body-meditation session was excellent – full of incense, music, and a kind of slow ballet of restful movements. Is this compatible with Christian prayer? I don't want to lose my Christian roots. But I have a gut feeling they might be in danger.

Dear Susan,

I think there are many in your position who have had a similar experience and yet don't see any difficulties. I agree with your instinctive sense of danger, even if it would be wrong to make a blanket condemnation of all the more experimental approaches to spirituality today. Personally, I learnt a lot from six months in India way back in the seventies. It gave me confidence in the Christian relevance of certain approaches to prayer that included the body, that united the Jesus Prayer with the rhythm of the breath, that taught various skills of stillness as I like to call them. Physically I never became very expert in yoga, but I did find certain exercises helpful as a *preparation* for prayer. They gathered the otherwise scattered self and I was more ready for the listening from the heart that is one key to personal prayer.

I underlined 'preparation' because on their own I don't think these 'methods' can count as Christian prayer. Indeed if they become ends in themselves, they leave out that sense of a receiving relationship with God which is a key element in prayer. If my 'mantra', for instance, stays on the level of self-exploration or self-awareness, it can forget the crucial Christian reality that we are first spoken to by God in Christ, and so all our spiritual efforts are responses to a gift, and variations on a long exchange of love – something first received and only slowly lived. (By the way remember that the author of *The Cloud of Unknowing*, the masterpiece of contemplative wisdom from medieval England, advised the repeated use of the word Jesus long before the fashionable word 'mantra' arrived from the East.)*

Certainly, in the chaotic rhythms of modern life-pressures many of us, myself included, need an antechamber to prayer. We need to quieten ourselves, to find ways of relaxing into an awareness of mystery. When we are 'all over the place' in consciousness, anything that gathers us can be helpful. But this is more preparation than prayer itself. That's the first distinction that I'd offer you.

Let me come to the New Age movement you mentioned. Go into any big bookshop and you will find more books in the section called 'New Age' than under 'Religion'. It's a new phenomenon in recent years, at

*See Letter 1 for a quotation concerning this.

least in the more comfortable world. Immediately I'd want to offer you another distinction – between 'New Age' as a theory and as a tendency. The theory is more obviously anti-Christian, and I don't need to go into it here. It involves such doctrines as reincarnation or a totally new astrological era, or events like 'channelling', which is really a new name for old-style seances, or forms of worship that verge on the neo-pagan, the superstitious or the magical.

But the 'tendency' is much more widespread than the theory, and perhaps more subtly deceptive. It is a new sub-culture with a lot of influence. Even if I partly enjoyed the film *Little Buddha*, I was left with the worry that it was an attractive form of New Age for children! Like the novel *Jonathan Livingston Seagull*, of a generation ago, it thrives on a 'soft' spirituality.

So by the New Age 'tendency' I mean a mood of openness towards anything 'spiritual', and indeed quite an explosion of writings and activities that try to meet this need. Perhaps because many have become disillusioned with an older materialism – both as a philosophy and a life-style – they are looking for alternative ways of meaning. There is a similar reaction against rationalism, and rather like the Romantic movement around the year 1800, there is a certain stress on inner journeys of the heart and imagination. All this is a relatively new note within the chord of contemporary culture – it was not foreseen thirty years ago when everyone was talking about inevitable secularization.

My hunch is that the hungers are genuine but the ways of answering them are often questionable. At its simplest some responses to these spiritual needs are dangerously lonely, and by lonely I mean they can lack roots: they can be cut off from the wisdom of history or of tradition, such as we have within the Church in spite of all its disappointing human failures. More paradoxically, perhaps this spirituality can be a new form of atheism. The old atheism was militant, like the rebellious Prometheus stealing the fire of the gods. But this newer tendency can be 'soft' and self-absorbed, like Narcissus falling in love with his own image. The older unbelief denied the 'existence' of God. The new tone is captured in this sentence from a typical New Age book: 'I seldom use the word God, as it has so many confusing connotations. I prefer terms such as higher power, spirit, or your higher self'. Such vagueness leaves no room for the personal concreteness of God in Jesus Christ. In fact often New Age talks about a 'Cosmic Christ', an impersonal energy, one of many such forces in the universe.

Am I being too harsh? It is because I want to alert you to possible deceptions. Perhaps the key question to ask is this: where are these New Age tendencies leading you long-term? Towards self-exploring of an exciting but private kind, or towards self-giving in the Spirit of Christ? And the important word there is 'long-term'. I have no doubt that your weekend offered short-term good and may even have given you a stimulus for deeper prayer. But if you get more involved in such occasions, is the gospel going to get marginalized in the *long-term*?

The opposite of being spiritually isolated is community. The opposite of short-term is a sense of history. The opposite of an impersonal sense of the divine is the incarnation of Jesus in the Gospels. The opposite of private 'spirituality' is social commitment. The opposite of Narcissism is prayer. I fear that New Age tendencies can offer many attractive, immediate satisfactions that pose as real fulfilments, but that they can miss those more challenging roots of wisdom: community, history, social vision. And real prayer which always involves an encounter.

If today's culture leaves people without roots, it is no surprise that many are desperate to find some inner anchors for themselves. But the journeying promoted by the New Age can avoid any struggle beyond the quest for inner comfort zones. Decades ago Aldous Huxley, himself a somewhat erratic spiritual searcher, saw some of these dangers: 'where personality is developed for its own sake, there tends to be a rising of the barriers of separateness and an increase of egoism'. So, if there is a god present in this closed world, it could be an idol which serves as an echo-chamber for our subjectivity rather than an icon which looks at us and calls us beyond mere self-consciousness.

Susan, beware of cheap answers to genuine longings. You need some of the skills of discernment to see through the short-term and to have the courage to follow the long-term and genuine road of faith. That's what I've been suggesting here. Adapting some famous words of St Augustine ('Seek what you seek but not how you seek it'), I'd want to say to you: seek what you seek, but not only how those groups seek it. Seek out a wavelength worthy of your spiritual needs, and a set of practices and disciplines that offer scaffolding for prayer. The New Age approach puts all the focus on the depths of the self, and therefore, it will prove a spiritual cul-de-sac. There are depths of the self but they are meant to reach out to God. With prayer as listening and as relationship (even in silence), there is a flow of contact with God. Or to put it in an image: without inflow and outflow the lake of spirituality can become stagnant and self-concerned.

In brief, you are right to look for nourishment for your hungers. You are right to opt out of trivial ways. You are right to want to learn languages of spiritual depth. But don't fall into the spiritual loneliness of forgetting that the adventure starts from God, not from you. Look for community, for concrete commitments, for ancient anchors. Within Christianity there is a long stream of wisdom about the inner life, which is sadly little known. Ultimately, if your prayer is Christian, it involves an encounter, in mystery, with the revelation of God in Jesus, and it is he who meets you and beckons you into a less lonely way and through the 'door' of his own humanity.

Letter 16

TO A NON-BELIEVING FRIEND

Dear Claudia,

This is going to be an unusual letter. You call yourself a non-believer, and yet you ask, 'What is it like to pray – tell me what you actually do, and why, and what happens? How can you always keep asking for things?' I can't reply to you from within my usual assumptions. A religious vocabulary would sound all wrong to you, full of pious assumptions. But thanks for the challenge, because that is what it certainly is.

Let me start with your last remark. Certainly, 'asking' or petition or desire is a strand of prayer, but not the only agenda possible. I seldom ask for concrete things for myself, like avoiding the 'flu or externals like that. I might ask to be worthy of various situations I have to face, especially involving the suffering or searching of others. Most of the time prayer is like a quiet resting with Someone, or a recognition of that Someone's Differentness and Goodness (called 'praise' or 'thanksgiving' in traditional language).

You want me to describe what I experience in trying

to pray, and what motivates the whole thing. I pray because . . . there are many ways of ending that sentence.

I pray because I believe God started it – the conversation I mean. Because if it is true that God exists and loves us, and reaches out to us in Christ, then it is only natural to want to remember that central relationship, and to nourish the heart's sense of gift. That's assuming a lot, I hear you say: yes, it's assuming the very core of Christian faith. So let me put it in more secular terms: once you discover a whole level of rich awareness, it just seems wrong to neglect it.

I pray because I gain strength from trying to pray each day. It is not always a success by any means: sometimes it seems empty drudgery, and sometimes I run away. But often enough, after some struggling to focus the heart, there comes a real sense of presence and peace. And I emerge more free to live and love.

I pray because I need to pray: if I don't, I have known myself to become superficial or even dangerous, at least in petty egoism and insensitivity to others. I can become addicted to all sorts of small compulsions – everything must be the way *I want it*. So, as Jesus put it, I need to 'watch' in order that the heart will not be coarsened by all the traps and tensions of life (Luke 21:34).

Let me come to 'what happens'. A movement of some kind – an 'exodus' from the false self, a slow liberation. Prayer often starts from the reality of the moment, which can be wonder or gratitude over some of the goodness I have glimpsed around me, but it can start with mere dullness, hurt, shadows, confusion, resentment. I try to gather whatever is this daily truth and bring it before Jesus Christ – who himself knew all that range of emotions, without my more selfish edges to them. What happens? Perhaps I am gradually enabled to 'exit' from the small story of myself and to expand and belong within the larger adventure that Jesus called the Kingdom.

I may have lost you there, have I? The Kingdom means a whole new vision, a life in tune with God, a slow way of energetic love. The Kingdom is meant to change us, and to create a different kind of world. In prayer I glimpse that larger-than-me invitation, that huge hope of God. There are 'bad days' when, at least from my point of view, nothing works, and frustration reigns from beginning to end in the time of prayer. It's usually my own fault – for not living with more generous imagination, or not preparing the ground more humbly. But when I try honestly to pray, more often than not I end up 'larger' than I began, more compassionate, and I hope more in touch with the depths of life.

What do I 'do' in fact? I often 'use' some passage from Scripture to begin with. It can be a phrase (like 'What are you looking for? Come and see'), or a simple moment in the Gospel (like recognizing the Risen Jesus on the distant shore at dawn). Years ago I used to take these biblical texts in bigger gulps. I would have a new passage each day for prayer. Now I find that I come back to the same short text again and again. It's like an anchor – providing some concrete way of awakening the desire and settling the scattered mind.

If it settles, fine. If it doesn't, that's another story: so many 'jumpy monkeys' can swing from branch to branch in the tree of the mind. That's an image a guru once gave me in India to capture the restlessness that can happen. But supposing the monkeys are peaceful, having some snippet of Scripture is more like a door into presence, into silence.

And here is something I would love to be able to

describe for you but it's next to impossible. Prayer at its best becomes a silent relationship, a being there, even a sense of fullness but without words. I'm no mystic but I have some idea of what the mystics are talking about. When I read the extraordinary poetry of St John of the Cross, I recognize the mood of the journey.

> On a dark night,
> full of desire, fired with love,
> (a joyful state)
> Out I went without being seen
> while all my household were asleep.

That captures perfectly the mixture of what is understood and what is not, the darkness, the love, the 'exodus' to a lovers' meeting, and the fact that the usual levels of perception are, as it were, fallen asleep.

Through the centuries it is no accident that people like John of the Cross have used the language of sexual joy to speak also of a sense of silent union with God. There is what the medievals called 'tendencia' followed by 'complacencia': in modern language it would be urgency of desire followed by restfulness beyond desire. For the medievals, they pointed to two wavelengths of love, one of them full of active seeking, the other overwhelmed with fulfilment, and wanting to stay there in stillness. Something of this adventure is echoed in my prayer – at least occasionally.

As I write all this, I'm very aware that behind it all there are basics you do not share. But you asked for it! Perhaps when I speak of God, you think I am falling into an attractive illusion, even a crutch that can shield me from reality. And even if you admit that there is something genuine in all this, from your point of view it can simply be a useful psychological exercise. Anyone who practises any kind of quiet or reflection for a certain time each day, will surely benefit from it. But where is the need to bring God into it?

I appreciate your doubts. And yet if prayer were only an escapist exercise, it would surely be easier. I experience it as a road of pruning that powerfully challenges the petty self. Those who say that religion is all a projection of our infantile needs for security can't have read the Gospels very closely. There Jesus disturbs as much as he consoles. The same can be said about the Christian way in general. As Nicholas Lash, a contemporary theologian, has said, Christianity is a school for taming 'human greed and fearfulness into patterns of attentiveness, detachment, peacefulness, and trust'. But he adds that what we learn in that school is 'given to us ... not invented by us'. That is what 'revelation' means. I'm sure you share in your own way the 'exodus' from egoism that for me is involved in prayer, but you do not see any Companion on the road with you. That is the divide between us.

But back to prayer in particular. The interpretation from inside faith is different. Any interpretation from outside misses a major key – the 'You' experience, so to speak. There are times in praying when I am surprised by something simple: I call it a sense of 'You', of God being close, and, above all, 'speakable to'. The very fact of being able to say 'You' changes everything. This 'You' that is God is like another person, even though totally different, mysterious, hidden, beyond the senses. A 'You' that addresses me, not necessarily in words, and a 'You' that I can speak to, with or without words.

As I go on, I realize that much of this may seem foreign to you. I have tried to tell things more or less as they are. It's not easy to do justice to something so simple as prayer (and yet in ways so complex), and to make sense to an 'outsider' as you describe yourself.

Rereading some of this letter, I fear it may give you a rather idealized picture. So let me end with a confession. Sometimes I only pretend to pray. I sit there 'giving time to prayer'. But nothing is happening. I have not even bothered to set the compass of the heart. It's not a mystical darkness but a lazy blank. But even those dis-graceful days can emerge into something of grace. As they say in Dublin, you catch yourself on. And turn humbly towards the 'You'. Prayer is remembering God, but often it is simply an exercise in basic and sometimes painful honesty.

Letter 17

BRIDGES TO REALITY

Christine writes: My friend Susan showed me your letter on the New Age. I share your doubts about that movement but I think you left something out. New Age is trying to offer a path to 'holistic' or integrated living. You said their desire could be right, but the answer offered could be wrong. True.

Over the years I've prayed, or tried to, and I've made one major discovery: the bridge between prayer and life is the key to Christian prayer, at least for people like me 'in the world', as you religious used to say.

Certainly I have to recall God 'directly' through times of explicit prayer, but most of the time I have to reach God through being a wife, a mother, a teacher, and so on. I get impatient when discussions of prayer imply that it is something cut off from reality. If you stress too much the need for creating inner stillness, are you not in danger of making prayer an escape, a private journey almost in the New Age sense?

Dear Christine,
You offer me a wise and healthy rebuke, or at least a reminder: never to separate prayer from real life. Certainly, as you say, there is a need for some withdrawal. Even Jesus invited the disciples to 'come away to some

lonely place all by yourselves and rest for a while' (Mark 6:31). The context tells us that there was so much going on that they had 'no time even to eat'. It's consoling to find that level of activism even in the Gospel, and I'm sure there is a spiritual meaning intended as well: that the disciples needed to nourish their vision and sense of the Lord away from even the pressures of their mission.

But you are so right: that need for special times should not divorce prayer from the realities we live. If that happens, we have escapist and not Christian prayer – as you insist. As Paul Tillich once remarked, 'the existence of religion as a special realm of life is the clearest proof of fallen nature'. That echoes what you say. Let me take it further and suggest ways of praying which heal that possible split.

If I talk too much about creating some kind of inner silence, it can give the impression, as you say, that to pray is to build some cosy space for self. But real prayer is something quite different. It is another wavelength of meeting the God whom I meet all the time in so-called 'reality'. I like your expression – to 'recall God directly'. Prayer is a more conscious language of remembering the One whom I cannot consciously remember most of the time. And yet what I do 'most of the time' and the spirit in which I do it, must be in fact my main meeting with God. In the same way, you would surely say that your main growth in married life lies in the ordinary rather than in the special. But it needs the special as well.

It is dangerously narrow to say that prayer is possible only in times of withdrawal. That is the point of your complaint. Prayer involves not just time for explicit prayer, but a whole adventure of attitude that can gradually shape anyone's life. Go back to basics. We are here to echo God who is love. Jesus is the One who shows us how. Prayer is where we learn to live like him, but that learning happens on two different fronts: in the silence of the heart, and in the chaos of reality. Or, in other words, in explicit prayer and in lived prayer. And they need one another.

I like what Donald Nicholl once said, that we throw away experiences instead of discerning the 'finger of God in the seeming chaos of the day'. Every experience can be recognized as the call of God. But it is an acquired skill to recognize the Spirit in the crowdedness of reality. How can one see God in the pressures of each day? How can one foster a spirit of 'lived prayer'?

I often long to be able to 'see God in all things' (a phrase of Ignatius Loyola). But I have tended to misinterpret it, thinking of it only as a kind of conscious remembering. It can be that. I'm sure that I can encourage the blank moments of the day to be more explicitly in contact with God. Waiting at a bus stop. Walking downstairs to meet someone. Making the bed. The day is full of such moments in neutral gear, times that can be wasted, but could, with a little effort, become more gently in contact with God. It's not even a matter of speaking to the Lord. It's more a matter of background music, a sense of doing God's will, or of trying to be in tune with the self-giving of Christ.

And yet this semi-explicit prayer, or prayer in the fragments of the day, is not the key to what I am calling 'lived prayer'. Lived prayer is lived. By its nature it cannot be conscious of God. It is not a question of attention. I cannot give my attention to God if I am trying to teach, or write, or listen to someone. But I can give my intention and my attitude of heart.

89

Let me gather what I am trying to say in a kind of argument.

1. Daily living is a key place of encounter with God.
2. It is there that explicit prayer, if it is genuine, produces fruit.
3. The Christian quality of our everyday attitudes is a form of lived prayer.
4. In terms of time, this kind of un-explicit prayer is our principal response to God.

How then can we build a bridge between a quiet prayer of presence and this fidelity to the gospel in the small choices of each day? The best answer I know lies in a renewal of the old idea of an examination of conscience, making it a prayer of awareness rooted in the concrete realities of this day. In this way it can be a prayerful pause to become conscious of the flow of the day I am living, and to adjust the compass of the heart.

Suppose you have a break in the middle of the day when you leave work and walk to some place to eat. With a little practice, you can use this time (preferably ten minutes or more) for 'situated prayer'. By this I mean a prayerful glance through the hours you have just lived. Notice the mood that dominates. Ask to see your attitudes as following or as resisting the calls of the Spirit. Give thanks for what was generous or in tune with Christ. Recognize humbly the moments when you became 'driven', or harsh, or out of tune with the gospel.

It's not a question of judging or blaming. It's not mainly a question of external behaviour. It's more like a musician striking a tuning fork to check that the instrument is really in tune, and to retune the strings that are not. It's more a matter of 'quality control' of your responses to what has happened today. Because in everything you have been responding to the promptings of the Spirit of Jesus.

But there is a battle zone that takes place within my attitudes. Have I been living with that simplicity and trust that Jesus speaks of and that he embodies? Or have I let myself forget and fall into some of my sub-Christian ways? If so, I ask healing for this forgetfulness. I ask freedom from this false tone and for reattunement in his Way. Because Christ is that tuning fork.

Crucial to this situated prayer is not only looking back, but 'praying forward' so to speak. What of the rest of this day? What do you foresee? Just as you can quickly scan the past few hours, so the imagination can zoom through the coming events. You pause on where you find some danger. In such and such a situation, you could respond 'out of tune'. You ask for guidance, for wisdom, but praying about the concrete scene that you foresee, or about the people you may have to meet, and so on.

The purpose of this bridging prayer is very simple. It is a practical way of reading the flow of the everyday in the light of Christ, and of learning to respond better to each ordinary moment. It may even help you to remember the Lord more often in the course of the day. But that is not always possible. The main fruit lies in a quality of heart and attitude that can guide your living. And so you respond to the Lord in the daily struggle of reality, even when you cannot think directly of him. You learn to 'do the truth' (John 3:21), but in the smallness of the daily. You trust that Paul's prayer can become true: through 'spiritual understanding' you become able 'to lead a life worthy of the Lord' – within the ordinary realities of your particular situation (Colossians 1:9–10).

Letter 18

ATTITUDE EROSION

Dear Reader,

I hope some of these pages have helped you in your way of praying. Trying to write these letters has challenged me to practise what I preach. Rereading them, I only wish I could always obey the good advice I offer! There used to be a series of language-learning books with titles like *French without Tears*. This little book makes no such promises. To stay faithful to some daily listening to God sometimes hurts. Because it means an inevitable erosion of our egoism.

That last phrase reminds me of one of the most saintly men I ever met, whose private hobby was 'coast erosion'. He loved watching how the ocean gradually changed the shape of the shore in local areas of the south of Ireland. Of course you could not see the change from day to day. But year to year yes. And he also delved into some specialist research about all this. I remember once helping him to track down an unpublished geography thesis dealing with Ballycotton Bay. He was a man of few words, but when he thanked me, he remarked, 'Coast erosion is like what God does to us, or could we call it "attitude erosion" '?

How can we change the attitudes that we spontaneously live from? How can we emerge from self into surrender? The erosion of the rock-hard core of ego is different for every individual. We are all slow learners of love, but with the goal of becoming more like God: free, flowing, giving life. It is a long Copernican revolution of seeing through the illusion that I am at the centre of things.

Prayer is not the only road of that erosion of egoism. I think that the ordinary demands of existence, whether in family life or of everyday dealings, can powerfully erode our refusals and teach us a new generosity of attitude. But prayer is a special place for heart-learning from God. From listening to a truth that is not ours, we undergo the 'pruning' that Jesus spoke of at the Last Supper. In prayer we realize that, paradoxically, this pruning is a liberation, an opening out to a gift, to a flow of living water.

Erosion sounds threatening only from the point of view of the rock. But from the point of view of the water, everything is different. With this in mind, I would like to end by reflecting on the invitation of Jesus to the Samaritan woman at the well:

'If you only knew what God is offering
and who it is that is saying to you:
Give me a drink,
you would have been the one to ask,
and he would have given you living water'.

(John 4:10)

Those few lines tell us so much about Christian prayer – in four movements.

1. We think of prayer as beginning from our asking, but here it starts with being offered a gift.

2. It then moves to 'Who', the person of the Giver, the One who approaches and asks for some little gesture. Perhaps for some minor erosion, some small self-giving.

3. Once you realize Who is with you, your hunger comes to life: in his presence you touch your need of healing. You need to learn love from the One who is Love.

4. Then Christ's gift will flow, becoming as he says a 'spring of water within'. Prayer opens you to a new presence of the Spirit (John 7:39). Even in the tangles of reality we can be rooted in a gift of consolation – lived more than felt.

Gift. Giver. Asking. Receiving. Four notes in the chord of Christian prayer.

But let us not spiritualize these steps too much. The gift of God takes flesh in this day, with these pressures, with these people. Here in the grit of the ordinary there will be many small erosions. Within this daily reality, the revelation of God continues. The same Christ 'speaks' in all these calls. And his living water is not necessarily some deep intuition or consoling grace; it can be the slow river of trying to be more kind, more pleasant, less self-concerned, which personally I find the greatest penance and the place where I most easily resist the erosion of God. But it is also *the* proof of prayer.

So prayer is a changing adventure, different every day. Pages like these can perhaps stimulate, offer a new perspective, suggest some practical skills, and ultimately give hope to keep going. But the day-by-day life of prayer is a costly and courageous *choice*, often against the grain of how we feel, and certainly against the grain of the culture around. It's easy to throw in the sponge. If these letters, written with real people in mind, could help others not to throw in that sponge, then this little book would be successful. In its modest way, it would be part of a slow revolution: an erosion of the small self and a stretching of the reach of the heart – towards the vision of God.

Postscripts

Under this heading I offer some fragments for reflection. They are like the compressed afterthoughts that one puts at the end of letters. Most of them are sparked off by the insights of various writers and theologians.

Generosity in others 'changes the lights for us', so that we begin to 'believe that we too can be seen and judged in the wholeness of our character'. This is George Eliot in chapter 76 of her great novel *Middlemarch*.

Prayer is liberated when I let myself be reached by the sheer goodness of someone else. But at the core of prayer is the generosity of God who changes the lights for us.

When I looked, I saw
rising
above the waters of the void
a star of the impossible.

And in my eyes it shone
and in my soul
like the appearance of Now
like the existence of Yes.

96

From the end of a poem entitled 'The Fable of Being' by the Irish Dominican poet, Paul Murray. A marvellous statement of the emergence from emptiness to gift.

'I hate to say most of these prayers written by saints-in-an-emotional-state. You feel you are wearing somebody else's finery and I can never describe my heart as "burning" to the Lord (who knows better) without snickering'.

How healthy is the scepticism and wit of Flannery O'Connor. I think she is the greatest Catholic fiction writer of this century, with a terrific sense of realism in faith. Here is one prayer she liked:

> O Raphael, lead us toward those we are waiting for, those who are waiting for us. Raphael, angel of happy meeting, lead us by the hand towards those we are looking for. May all our movements be guided by your Light and transfigured with your joy ... Remember the weak, you who are strong, you whose home lies beyond the region of thunder, in a land that is always peaceful, always serene and bright with the resplendent glory of God.

'Our soul is constantly clamorous with noise, but there is one point in it which is silence ... When the silence of God joins the silence which is secretly present in us, from then on we have our treasure and our heart in God' (Simone Weil).

Prayer comes from that meeting between the steady silence of God and our unsteady and resisted silence.

'Faith's imagination composes reality with irony. Who has the real power? Appearance will say the powerful have power, but the beatitudes and the sermon on the mount in the Gospel of St Matthew say the opposite. Like the imagination itself, faith moves below appearances into existence' (William Lynch).

So does prayer. A journey from surfaces into reality. And its fruit can be to share the irony of God, a divine comedy, smiling at folly.

Wendy Beckett writes,

> The simplicity of prayer seems to be the last thing most of us either know or want to know ... Prayer is not concerned with me, but with God. The essential act of prayer is to stand unprotected before God. What will God do? He will take possession of us ... [but] we keep a deathly hold on our own autonomy ... Prayer is the utterly ruthless test of your sincerity. It is the one place in the world where there is nowhere to hide. That is its utter bliss – and its torment.

Yes, prayer is the opposite of armour. But it can become a zone of shields. It's easy to do one's duty, put in an appearance, and forget the cost of nakedness.

Perhaps as life goes on, prayer is less about me – a matter of seeking strength or consolation – and more for God's sake, a purer adoration. I become less central. The glory of God comes into focus, and serving that glory also means nourishing the aliveness of God's people.

Intimacy with the Holy Spirit cancels out the spectator's uninvolved objectivity, with its external, critical attitude to the truth, and replaces it with an attitude which one can only describe as prayer ...

If we love we shall never turn away from contemplation, we shall thirst for it more and more. In prayer God gives himself to us (something we understand much better through practising the love of our neighbour), and, being thus filled by God, we are empowered to perform new acts of joyful, selfless love. Through love, contemplation is drawn into the mystery of transformation. (Hans Urs von Balthasar)

I often start outside and only slowly find a way in. It's a daily conversion from mastery to mystery. Mastery has me at the centre. Mystery has Love as centre. Or rather two loves, one as gift and one as flow. Liberating us that we may liberate others.

'They forgot ... They forgot ... But the Lord remembered' (Psalm 106).

That is the constant drama, which a spiritual life tries to confront. We forget who we are, who God is, the goal of the heart. But prayer is the art of remembering, and it has two moods or keys – like a piece of music.

One remembering is conscious. It shapes the heart by looking at the Lord, receiving in silence. The other remembering is lived and often not conscious. It echoes Christ in the options of each day, against the background music of the Spirit's coaxing.

Real growth happens in the flow between these two: the mysterious vulnerability of prayer and the slow learning-of-love in the theatre of the ordinary. Together they mean a long passover from ego to servanthood with Christ.